That Determine Your Destiny

Yan Hadley

New Life Publications

New Life Publications
45 Heatherbrook Road
Anstey Heights
Leicester LE4 1AL
Tel: 0116 2356992

Copyright © 2003 Yan Hadley

All rights reserved. No part of this publication may be reproduced, stored in any retrieval system, or transmitted, in any form or by any means, electronic, mechanical, photocopying, recording or otherwise, without the prior permission of the Publisher.

Short extracts may be used for review purposes.

Unless otherwise stated all Scripture quotations are from the Revised Standard Version of the Bible. Copyright © 1946, 1952 by the division of Christian Education of the National Council of the Churches of Christ in the United States of America.

A V - Authorised Version. Crown copyright.

Amp - Amplified Bible. Old Testament copyright © 1965, 1987 by the Zondervan Corporation. The Amplified New Testament © copyright 1958, 1987 by the Lockman Foundation.

NIV - The Holy Bible, New International Version. Copyright © 1973, 1978, 1984 by International Bible Society.

ISBN: 0 9531107 29

Production by: Moorley's Print & Publishing,
23 Park Road, Ilkeston, Derbys DE7 5DA
utilising data supplied on disk

Published by: New Life Publications, Leicester

Dedication

This book marks the celebration of my 25 years in 'full-time' Christian ministry and is dedicated to each of our prayer partners who so faithfully continue to support the work.

The help they give is vital, in fact, without God working through such people this ministry could not exist and I am therefore deeply grateful. It is my sincere prayer for them, and readers of this book, that they might fully discover and pursue the destiny to which God has called them.

Contents

	Acknowledgements	6
	Introduction	7
Ch 1	Choosing To Believe You Have A God-Given Destiny	9
Ch 2	Choosing To Rest Secure In God's Sovereignty	31
Ch 3	Choosing To Develop Divine Dimensions	51
Ch 4	Choosing To Find Fulfilment In God	75
Ch 5	Choosing To Live By The Transforming Power Of Faith	97
Ch 6	Choosing To Be Free From The Ruin Of Regrets	113
Ch 7	Choosing To Trust In The Power Of The Blood	133
Ch 8	Choosing To Advance In Times Of Adversity	153
Ch 9	Choosing To Prepare For Revival	173
	Other Publications	192

Acknowledgements

My thanks go to everyone who has encouraged me and played a part in seeing this, my fifth book, published. I gladly acknowledge the kindness and commitment of good friends who have kept me motivated in what has been an extremely difficult period of my life.

Particular thanks also go to those who have sacrificed their own time in meticulously proof-reading the manuscript:

Helen Cockram in Cheshire, Jo Fraser in Berkshire, and Becky Rock in Lincolnshire.

Cover photo image © Frank Whitney/Brand X Pictures/ PictureQuest - used under Licence"

Introduction

A certain courthouse in Ohio stands in a unique location. Raindrops that fall on the north side of the building go into Lake Ontario and the Gulf of St. Lawrence, while those falling on the south side go into the Mississippi River and the Gulf of Mexico. At precisely the point where the peak of the roof is positioned, just a gentle puff of wind can determine the destiny of those raindrops. It will make a difference of more than 2,000 miles to their final destination.

Thankfully, the destiny of you and me is not so haphazard, though it is significantly affected by what might at times seem to be quite trivial. The future of our lives is not determined by 'chance' factors around us, but it is determined by the every day decisions, both big and small, that we choose to make.

This book is a sequel to my previous publication, "Realising Your Full Potential", and seeks to emphasise some of those areas where our choices shape the person we become. These godly decisions are what enable us to discover an incredible adventure in the pursuit of our destiny.

The most important choice anyone can make, affecting the direction of their lives, is to yield themselves to Christ and follow Him as Lord. Becoming a Christian, though, is only the beginning of a brand new life. Each day, after the moment when we are 'born again', we make decisions that have consequences, not just for eternity, but also in the here and now.

To fully discover all that God has planned for us, we must take seriously the fundamental responsibility, which rests in our own hands, of making righteous choices. Indecisiveness is not an option for someone wanting to fulfil his or her destiny because even hesitancy has its own consequences.

Former president, Ronald Reagan, discovered this at an early age when his aunt took him to a cobbler for a pair of new shoes. The cobbler asked young Reagan, "Do you want square toes or round toes?" Unable to decide, Reagan didn't answer, so the cobbler gave him a few days. Some time later the cobbler saw

Reagan on the street and asked him again what kind of toes he wanted on his shoes. Reagan still couldn't decide, so the shoemaker replied, "Well, come by in a couple of days and your shoes will be ready."

When the future president returned to the store, he found one square-toed and one round-toed shoe! "This will teach you never to let people make decisions for you," the cobbler said to his dithering customer." "I learned right then and there," Reagan said later, "if you don't make your own decisions, someone else will!"

In view of the fact that we have been created for a purpose, and called by the God of the Universe to discover what He has ordained for our lives, we ought to be decisive in everything we do. He has fashioned us with a dream and a future that we must pursue passionately. It is my prayer that as you read through the pages of this book, you might be challenged and encouraged to live your life to the maximum.

One man who intended to do so, though not at all with God in mind, was the Irish novelist and playwright, George Bernard Shaw. Although an outspoken atheist the sentiment he expressed is admirable and noteworthy, if not somewhat hollow:

> "I am of the opinion that my life belongs to the whole community and as long as I live, it is my privilege to do for it whatever I can. I want to be thoroughly used up when I die. I rejoice in life for its own sake. Life is no brief candle to me. It is a sort of splendid torch which I've got hold of for the moment, and I want to make it burn as brightly as possible before handing it on to future generations."

Eloquent words, but how much more meaningful our lives can be when the decisions we make issue out of a desire to please God:

> *"Trust in the Lord with all your heart, and do not rely on your own insight. In all your ways acknowledge Him and He will make straight your paths."* (Proverbs 3:5 & 6)

Chapter 1

Choosing To Believe You Have A God-Given Destiny

The day our grandson was born was one of the most profound experiences of my life. I was actually there, at the birth and it was an amazing feeling. To be present when both our daughters were delivered into the world was wonderful, but to witness my child's own child being born was an awesome occasion that I'll never forget. Gazing at the miracle of that small, precious bundle, I couldn't help but look back to what seemed only like yesterday when I held my daughter and prayed she would discover God's plan for her own life. I remember contemplating then, nearly 18 years ago, the potential of that small infant, and could only dream of all she might become. Now I was holding my grandson, reflecting on the same thing. Here was a new life; one no doubt with many hazards in front of it but also with unlimited opportunities and possibilities that the years ahead would unfold.

In sad and stark contrast to this, the most heart-rending feeling I've known was to be at the hospital bedside of my father suffering with Senile Dementia. Advanced in age and with his memory all but gone, he was at the end of his days; a frail, empty shadow of himself; a man who, throughout his 78 years, had chosen to leave God out of his life.

For some people, misfortune or ill health has robbed them of any further chance to fulfil their potential and they are all too aware of their missed opportunities and failures. Others are proud and self-confident; preoccupied with their own achievements, they think their life is important because of what they have accomplished or acquired. In the light of eternity though, any person who has pursued fulfilment and ambitions, but decided to ignore God, is left with the same pointless conclusion of a meaningless life. Their end is identical; as an Italian proverb says, "Once the game is over, the King and the Pawn go back into the same box."

The Bible gives a clear perspective on those who, in their search for success, have lived independently of God. It says,
> *"For what does it profit a man, to gain the whole world and forfeit his life?"* (Mark 8:36)

None of us are here on earth merely for our own fulfilment and excitement. Nor, having said that, were our lives ever intended to be ordinary, colourless, and mediocre.

Our expectation, in terms of destiny, is based on the fact that we have been made in the *"image and likeness of God."* (Genesis 1:26). There is greatness and creativity within every individual; something that is not simply the result of an imagined evolutionary process, but we are creatures with a soul made up of divine substance.

William Jennings Bryan, who lived from 1860-1925, was a God-fearing man and a great orator, political leader and lawyer in America. He became the nation's most prominent figure in the fundamentalist crusade against the theory of evolution and often boldly stated: **"The Rock of Ages is more important than the age of rocks!"** Bryan offered $100 in cash, which in those days was a considerable amount of money, to anyone who would sign an affidavit declaring that they were personally descended from an ape! Needless to say, nobody ever stepped forward to do so.

The superiority of man is presented in the Bible as being beyond the capability of any other living thing. This is seen in God's instructions to Adam at the beginning of creation when He said,
> *"...Be fruitful and multiply, and fill the earth, and subdue it; and have dominion over the fish of the sea and over the birds of the air and over every living thing that moves upon the earth."* (Genesis 1:28)

We are 'three-dimensional beings'; every person has a mind that needs educating, a body that needs feeding and clothing, but also a soul that needs God. As true as this is, it is in the sinful nature of man to think that his destiny rests entirely in his own hands. He believes that all he needs to do is carefully to plan his life and it will be full and fruitful. However, Jeremiah 10:23b says, *".... it is not in man who walks to direct his steps."* A person may think that they are the masters of their own destiny, but in doing so they make a grave mistake.

The Bible warns us that, *"There is a way which seems right to a man, but its end is the way of death."* (Proverbs 16:25). With this in mind, let us consider three important things about our destiny:

Firstly, The Purpose Of God For Our Lives

If we are to achieve our destiny, we need to have a driving force motivating us otherwise we get nowhere. The single-mindedness of the salmon fish is a good example. They are remarkable creatures with an amazing sense of direction; some of them travel as far as 2,000 miles to find the exact stream in which they were born. Somehow they know the precise destination they must go in order to lay their eggs. They are known as fish with fighting spirit and will battle against the current to go upstream and reproduce before they die. They not only have to conquer the strength of the river, but also avoid bears on both sides of the stream trying to stop their most important accomplishment. It is an extraordinary achievement as they overcome the rapids, rocks and predators to reach their destiny.

The same tenacity and instinctive, compelling sense of purpose can be seen with other species in the animal kingdom. It should not surprise us, therefore, that mankind, the pinnacle of God's creation, is also born with an innate destiny to fulfil; one that is placed within them by the Lord Himself: *"...God has placed eternity into man's mind..."* (Ecclesiastes 3:11b). Our lives remain incomplete until we are moving towards that God-given objective.

Destiny is that which our Creator has preordained for our lives; it is what He has predetermined us to do and become. Every individual is unique and special. None of us are an 'accident', nor do we come into this world taking God by surprise; He already has a plan and purpose for each person. His Word tells us,

> *"For I know the plans I have for you, says the Lord, plans for welfare and not for evil, to give you a future and a hope."*   (Jeremiah 29:11)

The shepherd boy and psalmist, whose destiny was to become King over all Israel, understood something of God's knowledge of him and became aware that a purpose was planned for his life. He said,

> *"... You saw me before I was born and scheduled each day of my life before I began to breathe. Every day was recorded in your book!"* (Psalm 139:16, TLB)

No doubt we can all easily identify with the words of John when he says, *"... it does not yet appear what we shall be...."* (1 John 3:2). The reality of this fact, can at times, be very discouraging and frustrating, especially when we feel progress in our development is slow or perhaps almost non-existent. God's purpose for our lives, though, will always be fulfilled, provided we remain patiently trusting His Word. The reassuring promise God gave to Habakkuk concerning his vision is just as pertinent for every believer:

> *"... Though it linger, wait for it; it will certainly come...."* (Habakkuk 2:3b, NIV)

His plan may not yet be fully revealed in our lives, but it is already clear and complete as far as He is concerned. This is more easily appreciated when we consider what happens long before the structure of any building is developed. First the architect *'sees'* and writes down his plan, then he gives it to the builders to begin work. All the details are settled before the first spade full of soil is removed; what is required is that those to whom the plan is given follow precisely the instructions written out. The same is true with regards to God's purpose for each believer. Before we were born His plan for us was in place. His blueprint for our lives included every detail necessary from start to finish. We just need to fully co-operate with that design in order that it might come to fruition.

Amazingly, God's Word reveals, He planned our astounding human potential and destiny even before our first parents were created, furthermore, central to that plan would be the Lord Jesus Christ:

> *"Who hath saved us, and called us with a holy calling, not according to our works, but according to His own purpose and grace, which was given us in Christ Jesus* **before the world began.*"*** (2 Timothy 1:9, AV)

Each Christian has to seek God for themselves in order to discover the specific, personal destiny He has for their lives. A good starting place is to see, in general terms, His plan for all believers and then diligently to live consistently with it. According to the scriptures the Lord's calling and purpose for us is:

(a) **To Be Like Jesus:** We have been predestined to be conformed to the image of Christ. God's great intention is to change the sinful nature we have to be like the nature of His own Son; to develop His character and ability in us so that we grow to be like Jesus. Paul makes this clear when he says,
"…. *For those whom He foreknew, He also predestined to be conformed to the image of His Son…"* (Romans 8:29)

When the apostle writes to the Ephesian Christians he also speaks of God's objective for the believer:
"…. *until we attain to the unity of the faith and of the knowledge of the Son of God, to mature manhood, to the measure of the stature of the fullness of Christ."* (Ephesians 4:13)

(b) **To Live A Life Of Holiness:** If we are to be like Jesus then having a blameless life is essential to that purpose. While we will never be 'perfect' this side of eternity, it is a necessary goal that we need to aim for and to pursue. As ambassadors of His Kingdom we have a 'high calling' to conduct our lives with integrity, in everything we do and say:
"He chose us in Him before the foundation of the world, that we should be holy and blameless before Him. He destined us in love to be His sons through Jesus Christ, according to the purpose of His will…." (Ephesians 1:4 & 5)

(c) **To Walk In Good Works:** In Ephesians 2:10, Paul speaks about the daily, practical outworking of our faith. He makes clear that it should be expressed in actions that others can see and benefit from:
"For we are His workmanship, created in Christ Jesus for good works, which God prepared beforehand, that we should walk in them."
This is not merely doing good, but discovering what the good is that God has already prepared for us to do, then putting it into action. Again in Titus 2:14 it refers to this

same purpose, but adds the need of being enthusiastic about the outworking of it:
> *"...who gave Himself for us to redeem us from all iniquity and to purify for Himself, a people of His own who are zealous for good deeds."*

(d) **To Live In Obedience:** When Peter wrote to the Christian exiles of the Dispersion in Pontus, Galatia, Cappadocia, Asia and Bithynia, he identified them as those, *"chosen and destined by God the Father and sanctified by the Spirit for obedience to Jesus Christ...."* (1 Peter 1:2). Obedience is a vital part of being able to fulfil our destiny. This is why we find the book of Deuteronomy is full of promised blessing, but throughout its pages the key phrase is, *"If you will obey...."* Obedience is one of the major factors that will determine what we accomplish for God in our lives, and it will always be costly. In fact, it would be true to say: "YOUR GREATNESS WILL BE DETERMINED BY THE CAUSE FOR WHICH YOU LIVE, AND THE PRICE YOU ARE WILLING TO PAY FOR IT."

(e) **To Proclaim His Praises:** God's calling upon our lives involves a personal proclamation of praise. This is not merely the vertical expression of worship to God that communicates our gratitude and love; it includes also the horizontal level of a verbal testimony, making known His greatness to others. As the hymn writer Fanny Crosby said, when speaking about the 'blessed assurance' she had of her own salvation, "This is my story, this is my song; praising my Saviour all the day long...." Peter also encouraged the Church about this calling when he wrote,
> *"But you are a chosen race, a royal priesthood, a holy nation, God's own people, that you may declare the wonderful deeds of Him who called you out of darkness into His marvellous light."*
>
> (1 Peter 2:9)

Secondly, The Power Of Choice

Eleanor Roosevelt, born in 1884, was the wife of Franklin D. Roosevelt. She gave tremendous support to her husband, enabling him to realise his destiny of becoming the 32nd President of America. In her own right also, her humanitarian efforts on behalf of the poor and oppressed helped her to become one of the best known and most admired women in the world. She was an outspoken advocate of social justice and felt a strong sense of personal destiny. Her understanding of the power of choice played a major part in the things she was able to accomplish in her lifetime. When referring to this she said:

> "One's philosophy is not best expressed in words. It is expressed in the choices one makes. In the long run, we shape our lives and we shape ourselves. The process never ends until we die, and the choices we make are ultimately our responsibility."

We all start out in life on the same basis and it is ***choice***, not ***chance***, that determines what we achieve. While our circumstances, upbringing, and opportunity all play an important part and can influence what we develop into, ultimately it is the decisions we make that significantly chart the course we take towards our destiny. God has given to us the power of choice; we have a free will and are not robots or puppets on the end of a string. We are, to a great extent, where we are in life because of the choices we have made. These choices affect the quality of our lives, the strength of our character, the extent of our achievements and ultimately where we end up. Many choices are made in life; some are trivial while others are critical. This fact may be a difficult truth for some people to face. However, when we realise it, we can at least take care that every choice we make is in harmony with God's plan for our lives.

All of us are living today with the consequences of choices we made in the past. These choices not only affect our own lives, but also those of our children and all whom we have influenced. J.B. Philips translates Galatians 6:7 by saying,

> *"Don't be under any illusion, you cannot make a fool of God. A man's harvest in life depends entirely on what he sows."*

A choice made is a seed sown and that seed will grow up and produce a harvest in our lives. Like seeds planted in the heart, the decisions and choices of the past have grown up to become mature plants, shaping our attitudes towards the future. This is why Satan works through the power of sin to impact our minds and tempt us to choose the short-term pleasures in life while forgetting about the long-term consequences of our decisions.

Carnality is making a wrong decision based on meeting a self-centred need, whereas holiness is the decision to choose what is right in God's sight and is motivated by a desire to please Him. An example of carnality is seen in the Old Testament when Esau, to meet a short-term passion, made the decision to enjoy a bowl of stew in exchange for the long-term blessing of his birthright (Genesis 25:29-34). Conversely we see in the New Testament, Jesus, in Matthew 4:1-10, made a godly choice to reject each of the temptations that the devil brought before Him: **The Lust Of The Flesh** – to turn stones into bread that would have met the need of His hunger after fasting for 40 days. **The Pride Of Life** – to throw Himself down from the mountaintop and prove that He was the Son of God. **The Lust Of The Eyes** – to rule the kingdoms of the world that Satan was offering Him.

Satan knew that if Jesus made any choice other than to reject his deceptive enticement it would destroy the purpose for which God had sent Him and His destiny would be aborted. Relentlessly, Satan pursued this aim against Jesus, right to the end, and in the Garden of Gethsemane Jesus wrestled with the prospect of the full agony of what His destiny involved. He was deeply troubled, even to the point of sweating *"great drops of blood"* (Luke 22:43 & 44, AV). However, it was during this intense time of distress that Christ made the most momentous decision of His life, one that would affect not only His destiny, but also the destiny of the world. He knelt and prayed saying,

"Father, if thou art willing, remove this cup from me; nevertheless, not my will, but thine be done." (Luke 22:42)

The power of choice is seen throughout scripture. In Deuteronomy 30:19 & 20 God explains that He sets two choices before us: one, a life of blessing, the other of curses and death. Having made this a black and white issue, He then, in love, counsels us to choose life so that we and our children might live in God's favour. Also, we see Elijah confronting Israel as they stumbled along in two minds regarding their commitment to honour the Lord. He did this with a question that demanded a choice:

> *"How long will you go limping with two different opinions? If the Lord is God, then follow Him; but if Baal, then follow him."* (1 Kings 18:21)

The danger of making wrong choices can have very serious consequences. One of the most challenging realities in the Bible is that it is possible to be called by God, raised up for a purpose, and even anointed by the Holy Spirit, yet miss our destiny by being distracted or diverted into making wrong decisions. Such examples are:

(a) **Saul:** God had chosen this man to be King and lead Israel out of bondage to the Philistines. When the prophet, Samuel, first laid eyes on Saul, the Lord said to him, *"... Here is the man of whom I spoke to you! He it is who shall rule over my people."* (1 Samuel 9:17). Samuel didn't choose Saul, nor did Israel at that time, rather God said, *"I have appointed this man."* The Bible goes on to say of Saul,
> *"The Spirit of the Lord shall come mightily upon you, and you shall prophesy with them and be turned into another man."* (Ch 10:6)

Samuel declared to him in verse 7, *"... God is with you..."* and Saul was transformed by God's touch upon his life: *"... God gave him another heart..."* (verse 9). He was to go with confidence, assured of the presence and blessing of the Lord. We therefore have here a man appointed by God, moved upon by the Holy Spirit, destined to lead Israel, and someone who was assured that God's presence would be with him. Nothing more could have guaranteed him success in fulfilling his destiny! However, while Saul started out well, and for a while lived in his destiny as he walked in the fear of God, it didn't last long.

Although Saul was appointed as King over Israel, one of the most tragic pictures in Scripture is when this man began to fall apart. He had walked in his destiny for only a short time, even though God fully intended that he would live out his days with the distinction of having the Lord's blessing upon all he did. Saul began to disintegrate, caving in to his need for human applause and acceptance. He made compromises to attain these things and in doing so the plan God had for him was lost!

Towards the end of his life Saul faced one of Israel's greatest military battles and his heart became fearful. He consulted with an evil witch at Endor, acknowledging, *"... God has turned away from me, and answers me no more, either by prophets, or by dreams..."* (1 Samuel 28:15). As a result of his sin in prostrating himself before her to seek help and guidance, God abandoned Saul, leaving him to die in shame.

(b) Samson: This man's destiny was known before he was born: *".... he shall begin to deliver Israel from the hand of the Philistines."* (Judges 13:5b). Angels announced his birth, giving his parents detailed instructions on how to raise him: Samson was to be a Nazarite, which meant in effect that he was to be given completely to God's service for his entire lifetime. He was never to drink wine or cut his hair and he was never to touch any dead thing.

Samson was raised under strict training and at a young age he experienced the moving of God's Spirit upon him:

".... the Spirit of the Lord began to move him at times in the camp of Dan between Zorah and Eshtaol." (Judges 13:25, AV)

He knew he had a destiny, that he was born for a purpose; and for twenty years Samson walked in the authority of his destiny. He judged Israel and he overwhelmed the Philistines, bringing hope to the Lord's people. God had planned to bless the rest of Samson's years with greater victories, but his destiny was aborted because he chose to please the carnal desires of his flesh in lust and sexual immorality. He kept up an outward appearance of righteousness, but at the same time chased after harlots (Judges 16:1). When he went down to see Delilah, he knowingly flirted with danger and he quickly lost the respect of his own people.

Instead of living out his days in honour, we read of him as a man who ended up one of the most pitiful weaklings in biblical history. In the end we see Samson strapped into a harness like a dumb ox, grinding away at a Philistine mill. His strength had gone, his eyes had been gouged out and he had become a laughingstock of the heathen; even his own people had turned against him. Samson's choice to continue living in sin cost him everything: his anointing, his freedom, his eyes, his dignity, his destiny and his relationship with God.

(c) **Solomon:** If ever there appeared to be a man of destiny and greatness it was this man. Early in his life the Lord said to him, *"My son, give me your heart, and let your eyes observe my ways."* (Proverbs 23:26). This was to be a pivotal directive for Solomon, one that demanded a daily, ongoing and willing choice. In his early years, as he responded to this challenge, he became the wisest, richest, most respected man of his time and his destiny was clearly laid out for him. He would be the King who once and for all would rid Israel of idolatry. Solomon promised both his father and the Lord that he would bring down every idol in the land, and for a while he walked in his destiny.

In 1 Kings 3:5-13, the Lord came to Solomon in a dream at Gibeon, offering him his choice of whatever He might give him and Solomon chose wisdom. As a result of that decision the Lord granted him wisdom, riches and honour and said that no other king would compare with him. This should have been sufficient for him to realise fully all that he had been called to do and to become.

Solomon's kingdom continued to grow in power, influence, strength, wealth and size over the course of the next few years, reaching all the way from Egypt to the Euphrates, the borders that God had promised Moses some 400 years earlier. The visiting Queen of Sheba was astounded at what she heard from Solomon as he answered each of her testing questions and she marvelled at the sight of everything she saw. (1 Kings 10:1-9)

As the years passed though, Solomon made carnal choices that caused him to wander away from God. The Bible tells us, *"King Solomon loved many foreign women...."* (1 Kings 11:1). This was in clear disobedience to God's Word (v 2), and the consequences of his choice eventually took their toll:

> *"When Solomon was old his wives turned away his heart after other gods; and his heart was not wholly true to the Lord his God, as was the heart of David his father."* (verse 4)

He amassed some 700 wives and 300 concubines, many from other nations, and to appease them he built numerous heathen temples in Jerusalem because they desired places of worship for their pagan gods.

Soon, the man who had been called to rid Israel of idolatry had become an idolater himself, and by his example caused many others to sin against God. He accompanied one wife after another to their temples, bowing before their heathen idols. Therefore, having written three of the greatest books in the Bible, the wisest of men died as the greatest of fools. Solomon ended up missing his destiny and concluded his days as a disillusioned, feeble and immoral man.

These great men certainly accomplished remarkable things and many commendable words might easily be said of them. At the end of their lives though, each one in turn could have no more accurate epitaph written on his gravestone than: ***"The Man Who Missed His Destiny."***

We have looked at the negative aspect of those who could have accomplished so much more for the Lord, and have seen the inevitable consequence of their wrong choices. There are also many positive examples in the Bible that show those who fulfilled their destiny because of their choice to make righteous decisions:

(a) **Joshua:** He had the awesome responsibility of taking over the leadership of Israel after Moses had died. To do this, having been in the 'shadow' of such a great leader for so many years, must have been a truly daunting task. God had promised him, though, that He would be with him just as powerfully:

> *"... as I was with Moses, so I will be with you;......
> for you shall cause this people to inherit the land
> which I swore to their fathers to give to them."*
>
> (Joshua 1:5 & 6)

This was his destiny and he was assured of success, but he was told in verse 7 that it would be entirely dependent on him being careful to make right choices, pleasing to the Lord:

> *"Only be strong and very courageous, being careful to do according to all the law which Moses my servant commanded you; turn not from it to the right hand or to the left, that you may have good success wherever you go."*

This is how Joshua lived throughout his life. His example to others not only caused them to be willing to follow his leadership, but also to respond to the challenge themselves of making decisions that would determine their destiny. At the end of his days he left them with a crucial decision to make:

> *"Fear the Lord, and serve Him in sincerity and in faithfulness;... and if you be unwilling to serve the Lord, choose this day whom you will serve;.... but as for me and my house, we will serve the Lord."*
>
> (Joshua 24:14 & 15)

(b) **Daniel:** Here was a person conscious of a destiny to fulfil; someone who would have understanding in all visions and dreams, a man who the Lord would use to challenge and influence kings. One of these would be Nebuchadnezzar, who would turn to God in repentance (Daniel 4:34-37). Another would be Darius; he would not only acknowledge the greatness of God but also instruct his entire kingdom to revere Him as Lord. (Chapter 6:25-27). Therefore, right from his youth Daniel chose to make personal sacrifices that made him stand out from his contemporaries: *"Daniel resolved that he would not defile himself with the king's rich food, or with the wine which he drank..."* (Daniel 1:8). He also refused the expensive gifts that Belshazzar wanted to shower upon him, saying,

> *".... Let your gifts be for yourself, and give your rewards to another...."*   (Chapter 5:17)

Steadily he began to ascend to positions of high office and authority. Throughout the reign of three kings he was appointed by them to be a ruler over the affairs of their kingdoms. Then, as he moved on to fulfil his destiny, he was faced with a major decision. Daniel was about to be made Chief Ruler over the whole dominion of King Darius when those around him became jealous, and plotted to make him choose between giving up his worship of God, or being thrown to a den of lions. Even when threatened with this terrifying prospect he refused to compromise his convictions. In fact, the moment he heard of the decree outlawing prayer to God, he immediately chose to open the windows of his house and make public his decision to continue. (Daniel 6:10)

The result of Daniel's choice to be faithful to the Lord and not concede to the pressure of others was amazing. Not only did he experience deliverance from the mouth of the lions, but the impact this had upon King Darius was so profound that the King made a remarkable decree to all the peoples, nations, and languages that dwelt in all the earth:

"I make a decree, that in all my royal dominion men tremble and fear before the God of Daniel, for He is the living God, enduring for ever; His kingdom shall never be destroyed, and His dominion shall be to the end. He delivers and rescues, He works signs and wonders in heaven and on earth, He who has saved Daniel from the power of the lions." (Chapter 6:26 & 27)

(c) **Mary:** This humble, young virgin woman was given the greatest destiny that anyone has ever received. She was chosen by the Lord to be the mother of the Messiah, the Saviour of the world. It is little wonder that her heart leapt for joy when the full impact of that calling dawned upon her. Spontaneously she burst out in thanksgiving and praise saying,

"My soul magnifies the Lord, and my spirit rejoices in God my Saviour, ... for He who is mighty has done great things for me and holy is His name."
(Luke 1:46-49)

As astonishing as this destiny was, its fulfilment, and ultimately our very salvation, was dependent upon her decision to believe God and be willing to surrender herself to His purpose. The likelihood of being rejected by Joseph her betrothed, being misunderstood by others and bringing shame upon her family as an unmarried mother, was very real. She decided though, to make the most important choice of her life and trust God. Initially Mary wavered because of the incredible nature of what had been revealed to her. However, after receiving some reassurance from an angel of the Lord she made her decision and said, *"... let it be to me according to your word."* (Luke 1:38b)

(d) John The Baptist: The Angel Gabriel was sent from God's presence to announce the news of John's birth (Luke 1:13). It was an event that was just as miraculous as that of Isaac and Jesus Christ, for he was born to his parents when his father was an old man and his mother well advanced in years (verse 18). At that time the moral fibre of his life and the purpose of his mission was not only revealed by Gabriel in verses 14-17, but his destiny was also made known through a prophecy given by his father, Zechariah:

"And you, child, will be called the prophet of the Most High; for you will go before the Lord to prepare His ways, to give knowledge of salvation to His people in the forgiveness of their sins...."

(Luke 1:76 & 77)

John was to be filled with the Holy Spirit from his mother's womb (verse 15b), and to speak in the 'spirit and power of Elijah.' He would have a significant impact on young and old alike, to,

"turn the hearts of the fathers to the children, and the disobedient to the wisdom of the just, and to make ready for the Lord a people prepared." (v 17)

His ministry was extremely fruitful. All the country of Judea and all the people of Jerusalem went out of their way to hear him preach, responding in large numbers to his message (Mark 1:5). John could have established a 'big name' for himself. However, in fulfilling his destiny he made the important decision not to let pride get in the way of God's purpose. Therefore, he took care that nobody confused him with the great prophet Elijah, and particularly that he was not mistaken for the coming Messiah (John 1:19-23). He chose to humble himself, speaking about Christ saying, *"... the thong of whose sandal I am not worthy to untie."* (John 1:27). This was an attitude he maintained throughout his ministry as he declared,

"He must increase, but I must decrease." (John 3:30)

John's message was clear and uncompromising, calling people to repentance. He challenged the religious authorities, referring to them publicly on several occasions as, *"a brood of vipers"* (Matthew 3:7). He even confronted the King about wanting to marry his sister-in-law, saying, *"It is not lawful for you to have her."* (Matthew 14:4). John's absolute commitment to his destiny was eventually to cost him his life, and he was beheaded at King Herod's instructions, but he fulfilled God's plan for him to the end. In doing so he received from the Lord the unique distinction of having a first class character:

"Truly, I say to you, among those born of women there has risen no one greater than John the Baptist...." (Matthew 11:11a)

Thirdly, The Practical Responsibility We Have

Sir Winston Churchill, who is widely regarded as the greatest British leader of the 20th Century, once said, "The price of greatness is responsibility." This is so true and is why, throughout every chapter of this book, the believer's responsibility in various areas is plainly emphasised. While our destiny is firmly in the hands of God, we cannot just sit back and expect that it will happen. Destiny is not merely something to wait for, but to achieve! We need to decide to make the commitment of working diligently and hard for what God has planned for us to become. As the world famous singer Luciano Pavarotti relates:

"When I was a boy, my father, a baker, introduced me to the wonders of song. He urged me to work very hard to develop my voice. Arrigo Pola, a professional tenor in my hometown of Modena, Italy, took me as a pupil. I also enrolled in a teacher's college. On graduating, I asked my father, 'shall I be a teacher or a singer?'

'Luciano,' my father replied, 'if you try to sit on two chairs, you will fall between them. For life, you must choose one chair.'

I chose one. It took seven years of study and frustration before I made my first professional appearance. It took another seven to reach the Metropolitan Opera. And now I think whether it's laying bricks, writing a book - whatever we choose - we should give ourselves to it. Commitment, that's the key. Choose one chair."

The Bible teaches us that we have an extremely important role to play in seeing our destiny fulfilled, which must be taken seriously. Making decisions is one thing, but being determined to fully see them through is something else. Paul wrote to the Christians in Philippi regarding this personal responsibility saying,

".... work out your own salvation with fear and trembling; for God is at work in you, both to will and to work for His good pleasure." (Philippians 2:12 & 13)

Peter also emphasised the same thing when he said,

"Therefore brethren, be the more zealous to confirm your call and election...." (2 Peter 1:10)

While most Christians desire to get from where they are to where they believe God wants them to be, there are some who are completely oblivious to any threat against their expected destination. It reminds me of the amusing story of a plane journey where the pilot announced over the intercom: "We have lost one of the engines, but there's no need to worry, it just means that we'll be arriving an hour later than anticipated." Thirty minutes later a second announcement was made: "Don't be alarmed but another engine has gone; we will be now be arriving 2 hours later at our destination." Not long afterwards the pilot apologised again, saying, "I'm sorry but our third engine is lost, so it will take us 4 hours longer than scheduled." At this point one of the passengers turned to her husband and said, "I'm starting to get really worried now; if that last engine goes we will be up here all night!"

In realising our destiny, we must be alert to the fact that there is a threat to the direction we want our lives to take. A personal battle must be fought because Satan's intention is to wipe out God's purpose for every believer. Jesus had already warned Peter about the way in which the devil would try to destroy his destiny; knowing then, from first hand experience, how serious this was, Peter warned other Christians about the same danger:

> *"Be sober, be watchful. Your adversary the devil prowls around like a roaring lion, seeking someone to devour. Resist him, stand firm in the faith…"* (1 Peter 5:8 & 9)

As real as this threat still is today, and while we must remain prayerfully alert, it should not cause us to become preoccupied with the devil's plans or power. Our confidence is in the fact that God has equipped us with everything necessary to see our destiny come to pass. All it takes to face whatever life or the devil may throw at us has been given into our hands. We just need to discover what these things are and live in the good of them. God's Word says:

> *"**His divine power** has granted to us <u>all things</u> that pertain to life and godliness through **the knowledge of Him** who called us to His own glory and excellence, by which He has granted to us **His precious and very great promises** that through these you might escape from the corruption that is in the world, ….and become partakers of the divine nature."* (2 Peter 1:3 & 4)

From these two verses we see there are three fundamental things that must affect our lives if we are to stand against the wiles of the enemy. God gives them to those whose hearts are receptive, and they enable us to develop into all He has planned for us to be:

(a) **His Divine Power:** When Paul spoke about the spiritual battle of every Christian, his emphasis was not on the devil's might or influence, but the supernatural strength we have, in God, to overcome. From the moment we are converted there is a realm of divine power, a dimension of dynamic ability that is available to us, which will transform and uphold our lives. Within God's power is everything we need for daily living and godliness. This is why Paul says, *"Finally, be strong in the Lord and in the strength of His might."* (Ephesians 6:10).

(b) The Knowledge Of Him: Supernatural power is very exciting but also extremely dangerous. It can be used as a subtle tool by the enemy to distract people, and lead them astray, away from their true destiny. Therefore, the origin of genuine power is stated as coming only through our knowledge of Christ; no other source is valid. When Jesus is pre-eminent in all things, then the *"eyes of our hearts are enlightened"* (Ephesians 1:18), and we grow in the knowledge of Him. This is something revealed to us by the Holy Spirit and is a 'heart experience', rather than knowledge we ourselves have developed through the accumulation of academic information.

(c) His Precious And Very Great Promises: When we are 'born again' not only do we have God's divine power energizing and equipping us, we also have His definite promises continually causing us to reach out beyond ourselves. They draw us beyond the realms of our own logic and ability. It is through these that we become *"partakers of the divine nature"* and escape from the corrupting influence that is in the world. These can only become active in our lives, though, when we value their worth; seeing them as *'precious'* and *'very great.'* For this reason it is impossible for anyone to truly discover the person God intends him or her to be unless they recognise the importance of His promises and appropriate them personally.

Peter tells us that part of our destiny is God's calling to, *"His own glory and excellence..."* (2 Peter 1:3b). It is a journey we are on right now, and in verse 5b he explains that because of this calling and all we have been given by God to reach our destiny, we must not treat lightly our personal responsibility: *"For this reason, we are to make every effort..."* (verse 5). This is not aimlessly striving, but a wholehearted determination to apply ourselves, with all diligence, to the practical role that is ours as we walk and work together with God.

Here the Greek word for 'effort' is *"epichoregeo."* In Greek drama, when they would stage plays, there was a combined contribution of at least three key partners. There was the poet who wrote the script, the State who provided the theatre and thirdly, a wealthy individual or patron called a *"choregos,"* which is the root word from which we get *"epichoregeo"* – 'effort'. The wealthy individual spent a lot of money and put in a tremendous amount of physical commitment, making great *"effort"* to ensure the play became a reality.

Peter in effect, is saying, that God has written the script, the world is the theatre where our lives in Christ are played out, but our diligent efforts are necessary to make the script come alive each day of our lives. The partnership of all three working together is vital to the final outcome; otherwise the script could be written, the theatre waiting, but unless it is accompanied by effort and hard work, the end result would be a failure.

Woodrow Wilson, the son of a Presbyterian minister, and the 28th President of America from 1913-1921, believed in the importance of hard work to accomplish those things that are important in life. He said:

> "Let me remind you that it is only by working with an energy which is almost superhuman and which looks to uninterested spectators like insanity that we can accomplish anything worth the achievement. Work is the Keystone of a perfect life. Work and trust in God."

The instruction to make our calling and election sure is something for each of us to heed. This does not accidentally or naturally occur, but it becomes a reality as we make a daily, sustained effort to add to the foundation of our faith 7 specific qualities. These flow from one to the other and are like climbing the steps of a ladder which take us towards our destiny of more clearly expressing the divine nature of God. By not stopping at any stage, but by adding one step on top of the other, we rise to the full heights that are possible for us to attain.

In 2 Peter 1: 5-7 we find what the progression of these steps are:

(1) *Virtue*: In an age of "anything goes," virtue is a rare thing. It speaks of courage and strength in having integrity of character and purity of soul. Our faith leads on to distinction in our faithfulness, which is expressed in a moral excellence and goodness where we choose to act in such a way that we reflect the sinless nature of Christ. It is a quality that improves not just the things we do but the person we are.

(2) *Knowledge*: This refers to correct insight, which keeps our lives balanced and stable. It is different from the previously mentioned *"knowledge of Christ,"* in verse 3, where the emphasis there is on a personal 'heart experience.' Here the knowledge added to our faith speaks of the effort '*we*' make to develop our minds in understanding more about the Lord. It is a knowledge acquired as we apply ourselves to learning all we can about God's character, His will and His ways.

(3) *Self-Control*: A life of moral excellence, and the effort we make to increase in our knowledge of the Lord, gives us an inner strength to have power over the 'Self-Life.' We master our moods and passions rather than being controlled by them, and in doing so keep our desires within the limits of what is honourable to God.

(4) *Steadfastness*: Bearing up under trials so that we do not give in, even when times are tough and discouragement is felt, is a characteristic seen clearly in Christ Himself and also in the early Church. It is a quality that enables us to hold fast to our goal in spite of opposition, keeping our eyes consistently on the Lord and His will.

(5) *Godliness*: The expression of our reverence for the standards of God is seen in devout conduct that comes out of devotion to Christ. It is a quality of character that stands out in an ungodly society. This becomes evident as we make every effort to have attitudes, values and priorities that are consistent with God's Word.

(6) *Brotherly Affection*: Sensitivity and concern towards other believers causes our motives to be pure and our interest in them genuine. We make a conscious effort to change our

manner so that the warmth of affirmation, encouragement and openness replaces criticism, pride, prejudice, suspicion, indifference, and defensiveness etc. This results in a desire to build up others rather than find fault and pull them down.

(7) *Love*: To brotherly affection we add love, so that we show no prejudice by relating to and favouring only the 'likeable.' God loves us not because we are loveable, but because He is love. With His divine nature inside of us we love in the same way: unconditionally, unilaterally and unreservedly. It is a sacrificial commitment that seeks the highest good of the other, putting them first without counting the cost.

This list, stating the effort we need to make, is indeed a 'High Calling' but it is followed by a guarantee from Peter that the outcome of having such a life will secure the destiny God has planned for us:

"For if these things are yours and abound, they keep you from being ineffective or unfruitful in the knowledge of our Lord Jesus Christ."   (2 Peter 1:8)

In conclusion: because we have been made in God's image and likeness, our lives can never be insignificant and should never be aimless. Each one of us have a God-given destiny. It has an aspect that is both general to every Christian, but also one that is specific to each believer. There are three things we need to choose to believe and act upon if we are to fully attain this:

Firstly - **The Purpose Of God For Our Lives:** Knowing we have a 'heavenly calling' which is clear, specific and substantial must become the central motivating force within us.

Secondly - **The Power Of Choice:** Accepting that personal choice, not chance, determines the person we become and the things we achieve.

Thirdly - **The Practical Responsibility We Have:** Realising the importance of not only making choices, but following them through with wholehearted effort, are the steps to a more fruitful Christian life.

Chapter 2

Choosing To Rest Secure In God's Sovereignty

During the initial construction in 1933 of San Francisco's Golden Gate Bridge, inadequate safety devices were used, resulting in 23 men falling to their deaths. For the final part of the project, however, a large net was placed underneath the engineers as a safety precaution. At least 10 men fell into it and were saved from losing their lives. Even more interesting is the fact that a 25% increase in work was accomplished after the net was installed. The reason for this was that the men now worked with the assurance of their security and as a result were able to wholeheartedly serve the project, without the distraction of fear.

Insecurity can become an emotional 'ball and chain' around people's lives, slowing them down and hindering them from achieving all they are capable of doing and becoming. It is a common problem for people and is always the result of failing to appreciate the greatness of God and the total commitment of His love surrounding our lives. For the Christian though, whose heart is set on fulfilling his destiny, insecurity is a pressure he can choose to reject by resting in the truth that,

"The eternal God is your refuge and underneath are the everlasting arms." (Deuteronomy 33:27, NIV)

There will always be restlessness in the hearts of those who are not secure - an anxiety and uncertainty as they strive for the approval and reassurance of God. It is for this reason His Word states; *"... there remains a Sabbath rest for the people of God."* (Hebrews 4:9). This is not a rest of inactivity but a reflective confidence causing us to relax, assured in the Lord's almighty power to enable us to fulfil His will. When God finished His work of creation He rested, not because He was tired, but in order to enjoy His handiwork. For the Christian, entering into God's rest means coming to the place of living in the good of all He accomplished, not merely at creation, but also ultimately at the cross, where Jesus heralded His victory over the devil with the words, *"It is finished!"* (John 19:30b)

Resting in God's sovereignty results in the believer having no need ever to be unsettled or anxious, because they live convinced that He is in control of every circumstance affecting their lives. There is an amazing peace that comes from believing, *"The Lord has established His throne in the heavens; and His kingdom rules over all."* (Psalm 103:19)

God is Sovereign over all things, including, **The Pervasiveness Of Instability, The Pressure Of Persecution,** and **The Personal Direction Of Our Lives.**

(a) **The Pervasiveness Of Instability:** Recently I heard the true story of a retired couple who, years ago, were so alarmed by the possible threat of a nuclear war, that they undertook a serious study of all the inhabited places of the globe. Their goal was to determine where in the world would be the place least likely to be affected by war - a place of ultimate security. They studied and travelled and finally decided to settle in their new home in the South Atlantic, on the Falkland Islands. However, in May 1982, not long after they moved, their 'paradise' was turned into a war-zone by Great Britain and Argentina; the biggest naval action to take place since the Second World War began and more than 1,000 men lost their lives.

Knowing security is an essential element of being able to pursue our destiny. Try as people may, though, their best efforts still leave them feeling insecure and anxious about many things, not least themselves, their loved ones and their possessions.

Every year billions of pounds are spent by successive governments trying to help people feel safe. We have a police force stretched to the limit in their attempt to keep law and order. CCTV cameras are in most main towns, schools, hospitals and even nurseries. Security firms are doing a booming trade and insurance companies have policies for every eventuality. To read in our daily newspapers of burglaries, muggings, rape and murder seem quite normal. Neglect and abuse of young children is also becoming more common and the elderly are no longer safe in their own homes.

Life has changed dramatically in just the last 40 years. As a young boy I can remember a time when my parents would always leave the house key in the front door all day, with never a thought that this might be a dangerous thing to do. Today, though, they wouldn't dare to be so carefree. All the evidence indicates that the perilous age in which we live is the *'last days.'* This period is described in the Bible as an era when, *"wickedness is multiplied..."* (Matthew 24:12), when *"Men's hearts fail them for fear."* (Luke 21:26, AV), and when there shall come, *"times of stress."* (2 Timothy 3:1)

(b) The Pressure Of Persecution: This atmosphere of civil disorder is nothing new; when the apostle Paul wrote about the insecurity of the age in which he lived he spoke of how it was intensified by religious persecution. This he expressed in a very vivid way saying,

"For thy sake we are being killed all the day long; we are regarded as sheep to be slaughtered."

(Romans 8:36)

You would think that such a prospect would be sufficient to make anyone feel insecure, yet in writing these words Paul conveys no fear or sense of intimidation. Rather his words express a positive note of confidence and are spoken in the context of being secure in God's sovereignty and love.

For the Christian living in the comfort of the 'civilized' western world, to be regarded as, *"Sheep to be slaughtered"* might seem a remote possibility. However, the gradual change in the trend we see towards greater violence and hostility is alarming. This is reflected in the proliferation and appetite people have for brutal films, loutish television programmes, aggressive video games, and malevolent children's books. The modern phenomenon of so called 'Road Rage' in daily traffic, 'Air Rage' on planes, 'Pedestrian Rage' in the streets and even 'Trolley Rage' in supermarkets also demonstrates that we live in an increasingly violent age. When we add to this society's hostility towards the gospel, that Jesus Christ is mankind's only Saviour, we have an explosive cocktail for religious persecution against our God-given destiny.

It is the Lord's intention that each one of us becomes secure in His sovereign ability to bring to pass His eternal purpose. We can be just as secure as Jesus was when a large and violent crowd, with clubs and swords, came to arrest Him in the Garden of Gethsemane. Peter tried to defend Him by striking out at the high priest's slave, but Jesus simply said,

"Put your sword into its sheath; shall I not drink the cup which the Father has given me?"
(John 18:11)

Jesus was able to rest, secure in God's sovereignty, knowing that the destiny God had planned for Him was being worked out, regardless of how it might have seemed to others.

Even when facing the terrifying ordeal of crucifixion, He was totally secure because He knew He was in the centre of God's will. Jesus had entered a place of 'rest' and, therefore, didn't try to justify Himself or defend His position in any way. Isaiah made known this security when he wrote about Jesus saying,

"He was oppressed, and He was afflicted, yet He opened not His mouth; like a lamb that is led to the slaughter, and like a sheep before its shearers is dumb, so He opened not His mouth." (Isaiah 53:7)

The only place of ultimate security, in circumstances of persecution, is in knowing our lives are, *"Hid with Christ in God."* (Colossians 3:3b). This is the most secure place on earth! By resting in God's sovereignty we express in our daily life that, come what may, God is in control and we do not have to fear anyone or anything.

David knew God's sovereign power was far greater than anything man could do to stand against it when he spoke of the Lord 'laughing' at people's efforts to dethrone Him. This laughter was not sarcasm on God's part, but an expression of the absolute absurdity of anyone trying to fight against His sovereign purpose and power:

> *"Why do the heathen rage, and the people imagine a vain thing? The kings of the earth set themselves, and the rulers take council together, against the Lord, and against His anointed.... He that sitteth in the heavens shall laugh...."* (Psalm 2:1-4, AV)

(c) **The Personal Direction Of Our Lives:** Throughout the previous chapter we considered the extraordinary fact, that by God's foreknowledge, He predetermined a plan for every believer. It was a purpose we needed to discover and work diligently towards. We can only ever do this, though, when we come to a place of being gripped by the revelation that God's ***Sovereign Ability*** is able to accomplish His ***Scheduled Agenda***.

An important aspect of God's sovereignty is seen in how He gives personal direction throughout our lives, to get us from where we are to where He wants us to be. In his book, 'Evangelism By Fire,' international evangelist Reinhard Bonnke recalls an outstanding example of this; God led him, when he least expected it, to one specific house in a city of ten million. It was an incident that changed his life completely:

> "In 1961, at twenty-one years of age, I completed my Bible College studies in the United Kingdom. I could then go home to northern Germany. The route took me via London. My train was not due to leave until the evening, so I had time to do some sightseeing. I just walked as my feet took me, without a plan, and somehow wandered south of the River Thames into the pleasant avenues of Clapham.
>
> Then, at a certain corner, behind a high wooden fence, I saw a name on a panel – 'George Jeffreys.' I had just read a book by this evangelist, and could hardly imagine that I had chanced upon the very house where the same man might be. George Jeffreys came out of the Welsh Revival and, with his brother Stephen and other members of the Jeffreys family, had introduced the full gospel message publicly to the people of Britain. His work shook cities, and tens of thousands witnessed mighty

miracles. Eagerly I ventured through the gate and up the path, ringing the doorbell. A lady appeared and I asked, 'Is this the George Jeffreys whom God used so mightily?' She affirmed it was so, to my great delight. I asked, hopefully, 'Could I please see Mr Jeffreys?' The reply was firm. 'No, that is not possible.'

But then that deep, musical Welsh voice, that is said to have held thousands spellbound with its authority, spoke from inside. 'Let him come in.' Thrilled I entered, and there he was. He was seventy-two, but looked to me like a man of ninety.

'What do you want?' were his words to me. I introduced myself, and then we talked about the work of God. Suddenly, the great man fell to his knees, pulling me down with him, and he started to bless me. The power of the Holy Spirit entered that room. The anointing began to flow, and like Aaron's oil, seemed to run over my head and 'down the skirts of my robes,' so to speak.

I left that house dazed. Four weeks later, like Elijah, George Jeffreys had been translated to glory. I had been led to see him just before he died."

The sovereign hand of God, that miraculously led Reinhard Bonnke from Bible college to meeting George Jeffreys, and eventually on to fulfil his destiny as a world wide evangelist, preaching to countless millions, is the same hand that guides your life and mine. This is emphasised in the Bible when it says,

"The steps of a good man are ordered by the Lord: and He delighteth in his way." (Psalm 37:23, AV)

Our security regarding the Lord's personal direction comes from the confidence we have in God's ability to finish what He has started; the belief that **His Sovereign Work** will ultimately bring to pass **His Stated Word**. Paul had this conviction when writing to others from a prison cell in Philippi, and he expressed it with the assertion, *"I am sure that He who began a good work in you will bring it to completion at the day of Christ."* (Philippians 1:6).

He knew from personal experience that God was bigger and greater than any opposition he might face and that his life was being directed by the hand of the Lord.

In Ephesians chapter 3, we find the apostle suffering once again in the cruel and uncomfortable environment of a jail, this time in Ephesus. His only crime, in the eyes of the authorities, was preaching the gospel, as he sought to fulfil his destiny. Outwardly it appeared he was a prisoner of Rome, confined by the will of man. As far as Paul was concerned though, he regarded himself as *"a prisoner for Christ Jesus ..."* (verse 1) - a man held by the will of God.

When our aim is to fulfil the destiny God has for us it will be costly, but by believing in His sovereignty, we can rest secure. In negative circumstances our view is always positive because, like the apostle, our response will be,

"What shall we then say to these things? If God be for us, who can be against us?" (Romans 8:31, AV)

This is something we consistently see with Paul. While in prison He didn't utter a word of complaint; there's not any sense of grumbling, nor even a hint of self-pity, or injustice; there's no feeling of, "Why me?" or "This isn't fair!". He was rejoicing instead in the midst of trial. A note of triumph was in his writing because he was secure in the knowledge that God was in control of his destiny. Therefore, even while being imprisoned, he could say,

"I have learned, in whatever state I am, to be content." (Philippians 4:11)

In considering these things we will see not only from Paul's experience but also from the examples of JONAH, JOSEPH & JESUS that when, **Deception Sidetracks The Proud, Difficulty Strikes The Faithful** and **Demonic Forces Oppose The Anointed,** God's sovereign plan and purposes continue steadily on:

Firstly, When Deception Sidetracks The Proud

Paul, who in his earlier years was called Saul of Tarsus, never ceased to be amazed at the wonder of God's sovereign power that had changed his own life. He had previously been a very devout Jew steeped in religion, but an outspoken blasphemer and violent persecutor of the Christian faith. As a young intellectual, schooled under the teaching of the great Rabbi Gamaliel, he was part of the strict Pharisee party and proud of his heritage, traditions and understanding of the Law.

Saul was determined not to give any ground to this *'new'* message concerning the resurrection of Jesus, and particularly that the Jews and Gentiles were one through faith in Jesus of Nazareth. He therefore hated the name of Christ and was blind to the truth of the gospel. Religious bigotry and pride was the cause of him being deceived and it resulted in a zealous attack upon the Church. He considered it his religious duty to wipe out what he believed to be a terrible lie that Jesus had risen from the dead.

This certainly brings home a very strong lesson to all, so-called, 'Defenders of The Faith' today; those who close their minds to anything that they can't rationalise or might feel uncomfortable with; people who because of their religious bigotry, legalism and pride, reject whatever doesn't fit into their tradition and who speak out harshly against anything that threatens their position. Such people are found, whether it's in Northern Ireland, the Middle East, or church life in our own country, where strife and division is caused over different views of scripture.

Although Saul was convinced he was right and that he was doing God's will in wreaking havoc among the churches, it took a divine revelation to show him his mistake. He had been deceived and sidetracked by his own proud heart, but God was greater than his pride and prejudice, and in a sovereign act, totally changed his life on the Damascus road. As a result, this man was converted from being a Murderer to a Missionary! – a Blasphemer to a Bible teacher!

Paul came to realise that the greatness of God's sovereign power was at work even before his birth, which is why he said, *"He set me apart before I was born …. in order that I might preach Him among the Gentiles…."* (Galatians 1:15 & 16). We see this again when the Lord spoke to Ananias telling him that He had a purpose for Saul. God instructed him to seek out the Church's fiercest opponent and pray for him to receive the Holy Spirit. This Saul needed in order that he might have the supernatural ability to fulfil the demands of his destiny:

> *"Go, for he is a chosen instrument of mine to carry my name before the Gentiles and kings and the sons of Israel; for I will show him how much he must suffer for the sake of my name."* (Acts 9:15 & 16)

Such an example should give us tremendous encouragement and the ability to 'rest' in God's sovereign power. This is especially so when we consider the hardened hearts of our loved ones - those who have a destiny but at present are unconverted or backslidden. Also people who may be standing against God's purposes in our church; adamantly they believe they are doing His will, but deceived by their pride and prejudice, they are resisting the work of the Holy Spirit. If God, by a sovereign act of grace, was able to change the life of Saul of Tarsus then nobody is beyond hope!

Jonah The Rebellious

Another outstanding example of God's sovereignty, working in the life of a proud and stubborn individual, is seen in the destiny of the prophet Jonah. This man's pride and prejudice led him down a path of disobedience and deception. God's purpose for him was that he should go 500 miles east to take a message of repentance to the people of Nineveh. Instead he rebelled and, deceiving himself, thought he could flee from the presence of God, by catching a boat going to Tarshish, which was on the extreme western edge of the known world - as far in the opposite direction as he could go!

He didn't want to obey God's will because of his prejudice against, what he considered to be, an undeserving, heathen city; Nineveh was a place full of violence and cruelty and its people a constant enemy of Israel. He knew that if he preached to them they would repent and God would forgive them (Jonah 4:1 & 2). If this happened, he would be made to appear foolish in the eyes of others, when his prophecy of judgement and destruction didn't come to pass. God's sovereignty is seen throughout this account in the most amazing way, by six miraculous interventions to bring Jonah's life into line with His purpose:

> **(a)** *"**The Lord sent a great wind on the sea**, and such a violent storm arose that the ship threatened to break up...."* (Jonah 1:4, NIV). Such was the severity of the storm that these experienced sailors were terrified; they

threw their cargo overboard and cried to their idols for help. Amongst all this commotion they cast lots to learn who on board was responsible for incurring the wrath of God. They discovered from Jonah's own admission that he was the problem because he was running away from the Lord. Jonah knew that the only solution was for him to get off the boat. He, therefore, instructed the sailors to throw him overboard into the raging sea, telling them that the storm would then cease (verse 12).

(b) *"The Lord appointed a great fish to swallow Jonah; and Jonah was in the belly of the fish three days and three nights."* (verse 17). By a sovereign act of God's will, this fish had been prepared and brought to the exact place necessary at precisely the right time, not to destroy Jonah, but to preserve Him and bring him to repentance. During, what must have been, an appalling experience inside this fish, Jonah reflected on his foolishness and called upon God in prayer.

(c) *"The Lord spoke to the fish and it vomited out Jonah upon the dry land."* (Chapter 2:10). At God's direction the fish did not just spit Jonah out into the sea - if this had happened, his life would have been lost and his destiny left unfulfilled. The Lord brought the great fish close to dry land, and commanded it to release the prophet; he was then delivered safely, if not conventionally, onto the shore.

Jonah, sitting on the beach covered in fish vomit, was given a second chance by God to return and preach to the city of Nineveh (Chapter 3:1 & 2). Although he obeyed, his heart was still not right because he continued to hold on to resentment towards the people, and had a grudging reluctance to do God's will. As he preached the entire city of 120,000, from the King down, repented and turned to God. This was much to the annoyance of Jonah (Chapter 4:1-11). Therefore the process of God's sovereign purpose continued on so that Jonah would not simply fulfil his destiny, but he would do so with a right attitude.

(d) *"**The Lord God appointed a plant**, and made it come up over Jonah, that it might be a shade over his head, to save him from his discomfort..."* (Chapter 4:6). The purpose of the plant was not merely to give the prophet shade from the sun but to demonstrate the Lord's sovereign control over the normal process of nature. God prepares the ground and also the seed then by a miracle causes the plant to grow quickly. Jonah is happy with this and glad of its provision.

(e) *"But when dawn came up the next day **God appointed a worm** which attacked the plant, so that it withered."* (verse 7). In contrast to the 'great fish,' we see here that even the tiniest of God's creation is also under His control and direction. Therefore, this insect is sent with a divine mission - to destroy the plant protecting Jonah. In doing this we learn that what the Lord has given He can remove just as easily, but such action is never taken without a significant purpose, as God later reveals.

(f) *"When the sun rose, **God appointed a sultry east wind**, and the sun beat upon the head of Jonah..."* (verse 8). Jonah was now uncomfortable and mourned the loss of the plant that had brought him shade from the sun. He was so downcast and angry about the loss of the plant that he even wanted to die! It was at this point God showed him the ridiculously distorted perspective he had. In his sorrow he felt more compassion for the plant, which came one night and was taken the next, than for the fate of all the 120,000 people in Nineveh (verse 10 & 11).

Through each one of these six sovereign acts, Jonah was confronted with the extent of his self-deception and pride and was taught that he could not run away from God's will; no matter how far he went he was still seen by the Lord. The demonstration of God's mercy towards him eventually placed him back on track and caused him to see the rottenness of his attitude towards others.

Secondly, When Difficulty Strikes The Faithful

Throughout Paul's difficult experiences in prison we see that he was more mindful about others than he was about himself.

His concern was that his suffering and imprisonment might cause the Ephesian Christians to stumble and lose faith and so he wrote, *"I ask you not to lose heart over what I am suffering...."* (Ephesians 3:13). Paul had taught them about the blessings and victory of the Christian life. He had emphasised God's love for man and how, as a child of God, nothing could harm them, but now he himself was suffering in prison!

Why bad things happen to good people is unknown; in fact nothing has so puzzled Christians as the issue of suffering, particularly when it involves the innocent and godly. If we are to fulfil our destiny though, we need to have the assurance that, even when circumstances seem to be falling apart and everything is standing against us, God's great purposes are still being accomplished. Paul's security about this is seen in the same chapter in which he spoke of himself as, *"a sheep to be slaughtered."* In Romans 8:28 he says,

"We know that in everything God works for good, with those who love Him, who are called according to His purpose."

Paul, in writing to the Ephesian Christians, wanted them to see suffering in the light of God's eternal purpose. As Sovereign Lord, He was able to deliver from whatever troubles the righteous were in and bring good, even out of evil. In spite of Paul's difficulties he knew God's plan was still being worked out. David also declared this assurance of ultimate victory with the clear promise,

"Many are the afflictions of the righteous; but the Lord delivers him out of them all."   Psalm 34:19)

Joseph The Faithful

The sovereignty of God's purpose is seen working through the many afflictions that Joseph experienced. He'd been given a clear sense of his destiny through two unusual dreams. They were not his own vain imaginings, but prophetic revelations speaking of his future. His work would be so significant that even his own family would bow down before him (Genesis 37:7-10). Though not fully realising both the suffering and the glory that this would involve, he was to be the one chosen by God to preserve the nation of Israel through a time of great famine. He would also, at the age of only 30 years, be exalted to be ruler over all Egypt, second only to the King. (Chapter 41:40)

This was the destiny the Lord had for Joseph, however, many difficulties lay ahead of him that appeared to stand against God's purpose: (a) He was hated so much by his brothers, who were jealous of him, that they wanted to kill him (Genesis 37:4,5,8 & 20). (b) He was thrown into a pit and then sold into slavery (verses 22-28). (c) During his time of working in Potiphar's house he was unjustly accused of attempting to rape his master's wife and jailed (Chapter 39:7-20). (d) While in jail for two years he was forgotten by the butler whom he had helped and who had promised in return, to help him as soon as he was released. (Chapter 40:14 & 15)

In spite of all his difficulties and disappointments, he believed that God determined the purpose for his life and it was the Lord's secret providence that was working quietly behind the darkest deeds of man. Joseph's confidence about this is seen in his words at the end of all his suffering, when he revealed himself to his brothers:

> *"And God sent me before you to preserve for you a remnant on earth, and to keep alive for you many survivors. So it was not you who sent me here, but God; and He has made me a father to Pharaoh, and Lord of all his house and ruler over all the land of Egypt."* (Chapter 45:7 & 8)

Joseph made this important point again to his brothers after Jacob, their father, had died. This was because they were anxious that now, with their father gone, Joseph might seek to take some revenge on them because of what they had done to him. He assured them though, saying,

> *"… Fear not, for am I in the place of God? As for you, you meant evil against me; but God meant it for good, to bring it about that many people should be kept alive, as they are today."* (Genesis 50:19 & 20)

He was secure about his destiny being fulfilled. Even though it looked as though his life was experiencing one disaster after another, his circumstances never affected his convictions. Joseph had the assurance that, *"The Lord was with him;"* - at Potiphar's house while he was on the way up (Chapter 39:2 & 3), and in prison while he was on the way down. (Chapter 39:21-23).

God is the Sovereign Lord and it is His hand that shapes our lives. We can liken our relationship with Him as a potter working with clay, moulding us into a vessel of honour for His purpose. This was Joseph's experience and was what the Lord revealed to Jeremiah when He said:

> "..... 'Arise and go down to the potter's house, and there I will let you hear my words.' "So I went down to the potter's house, and there he was working at his wheel. And the vessel he was making of clay was spoiled in the potter's hand, and he reworked it into another vessel, as seemed good to the potter to do."
>
> (Jeremiah 18:2-4)

Corrie Ten Boom spoke of how, through the many difficulties of her life, she came to understand something of God's sovereign plan at work behind life's disappointments and discouragements. She expressed her discovery of this using the imagery of God, not as a potter, but a master weaver. Reflecting on this gave her an ever-widening view of how the Lord's workings, in every circumstance and every hardship, fit into His grand scheme:

> "My life is but a weaving, between my God and me,
> I do not choose the colours, he worketh steadily.
> Oftimes He weaveth sorrow, and I in foolish pride,
> forget He sees the upper, and I the underside.
> Not till the loom is silent, and shuttles cease to fly,
> will God unroll the canvas and explain the reason why.
> The dark threads are as needful
> in the skilful Weaver's hand,
> as the threads of gold and silver
> in the pattern He has planned."

Thirdly,
When Demonic Forces Oppose The Anointed

We now come to the very heart of God's sovereign purpose, a plan that all the forces of hell rose up to oppose. Paul speaks of this in Ephesians 3:9b, referring to it as, *"...the plan of the mystery hidden for all ages in God who created all things...."*

The 'mystery' Paul had received and the message he was called to make known was twofold:

(a) **The Restoration Of God's Divine Order:** This is seen in Ephesians 1:9 & 10: *"...the mystery of His will, according to His purpose which He set forth in Christ as a plan for the fullness of time, to unite all things in Him, things in heaven and things on earth."* At the beginning of creation, God, as Sovereign Lord, planned a Kingdom that would be made up of those submitted to His government and living in harmony with His will. This was something Satan destroyed when he deceived Eve and through sin brought disorder into the world.

God however, in spite of all the ensuing chaos that sin has caused, is working out His purpose to restore unity and peace in His creation. He revealed this ongoing intention through the prophet Isaiah, saying of Christ,
"For to us a child is born, to us a son is given; and the government will be upon His shoulder.... Of the increase of His government and peace there will be no end...." (Isaiah 9:6 & 7)

(b) **The Revelation Of God's Divine Wisdom:** In Ephesians 3:10 this mystery is further explained: *"... that through the church the manifold wisdom of God might now be made known to the principalities and powers in heavenly places."* God's purpose, for the world and for the universe, is centred in Christ the 'Anointed One' and in His triumphant anointed Church.

Jesus came, not only to end the devil's control over man's destiny and restore peace, but also to raise up a people who, anointed by His power to proclaim God's victory over Satan, are examples of His wisdom and grace. Isaiah expresses the determination He has to accomplish this in saying, *"... The zeal of the Lord of hosts will do this."* (Isaiah 9:7b). The same determination was stated by Jesus when He declared,
".... I will build my Church; and the gates of hell shall not prevail against it." (Matthew 16:18, AV)

Jesus The Anointed

In Christ the full glory of God's wisdom is made manifest. Without doubt, the most remarkable example of the Lord's sovereignty throughout scripture is seen in His great plan of salvation, which was established in Jesus who came as, *"... the Lamb slain from the foundation of the world."* (Revelation 13:8b, AV). It doesn't get more amazing than this!

Way back in eternity past, before the world began, Satan rose up against God and was cast out of heaven (Isaiah 14:12-15). From that point on he was set on destroying God's creation. This he thought he had achieved in the Garden of Eden, bringing a curse upon mankind. God though, even then in His sovereign purpose, had already made provision to remedy such a disaster. Prophetically He said to Satan,

> *"I will put enmity between you and the woman, between your offspring and her seed; He shall bruise your head, and you shall bruise His heel."* (Genesis 3:15)

While the devil would strike at the 'heel' of Jesus and for a short while, at the cross, halt His 'walk', Jesus, the offspring of Eve, would strike a fatal blow against the devil that would bring about his ultimate destruction. The prophets of old foretold the fulfilment of this event in the coming of Christ, God's Anointed One. This promise was later made known to Mary by the angel, who said,

> *"And behold, you will conceive in your womb and bear a son, and you shall call His name Jesus. He will be great, and will be called the Son of the Most High; and the Lord God will give to Him the throne of His father David, and He will reign over the house of Jacob forever; and of His kingdom there will be no end."*
> (Luke 1:31-33)

Through the seed of the first woman, Eve, God's sovereign greatness is remarkably displayed in the prophecies about Jesus which came to pass regarding:

(a) **The Purity Of His Conception:** The virgin birth and divine, immaculate conception was clearly foretold by the prophet Isaiah over seven hundred years before the event: *"... a virgin shall conceive, and bear a son, and shall call*

His name Immanuel." (Isaiah 7:14b, AV). To prepare Mary for the fulfilment of this awesome moment an angelic messenger said to her,

> *"... The Holy Spirit will come upon you, and the power of the Most High will overshadow you; therefore the child to be born will be called holy, the Son of God."* (Luke 1:35)

Joseph also was given the reassurance that he needed when the angel said to him,

> *"... do not fear to take Mary as your wife, for that which is conceived in her is of the Holy Spirit...."*
> (Matthew 1:20b)

(b) The Place Of His birth: Of all the nations in the world into which the Messiah could have been born, it was the parched, barren and insignificant land of Palestine! Not Jerusalem the royal city, but Bethlehem, which was *"little"* among the many towns and villages in Judah (Micah 5:2a). Further details of this location were given to the shepherds in that region who were told to look for Him in a humble stable:

> *"And this will be a sign for you: you will find a babe wrapped in swaddling cloths and lying in a manger."* (Luke 2:12)

As Paul reflected on God's sovereign hand in all this, he shows that the timing of Christ's birth was not a haphazard event, but part of the carefully unfolding plan of God:

> *"When the time had fully come, God sent forth His Son, born of a woman, born under the law...."*
> (Galatians 4:4)

(c) The Purpose Of His Mission: That which was planned from the beginning and revealed through the prophets is made clear in the words God spoke through Isaiah saying,

> *"The Spirit of the Lord God is upon me, because the Lord has anointed me to bring good tidings to the afflicted, He has sent me to bind up the brokenhearted, to proclaim liberty to the captives, and the*

opening of the prison to those who are bound; to proclaim the year of the Lord's favour...."
(Isaiah 61:1 & 2)

This came to pass when Jesus was 30 years of age. He stood up in the synagogue and read from the book of Isaiah, then said, to everyone's astonishment, *"Today this scripture has been fulfilled in your hearing."* (Luke 4:21)

When the prophet Micah was speaking of the miracle that would come out of Bethlehem he also announced the purpose of Christ's mission in saying, *"... from you shall come forth for me one who is to be ruler in Israel, whose origin is from old, from ancient days."* (Micah 5:2b). Another glimpse regarding the mission of Christ is seen in the statement of the angel to Joseph about his betrothed:

"She will bear a son, and you shall call His name Jesus, for He will save His people from their sins."
(Matthew 1:21)

(d) The Person Who Would Betray Him: God's Word reveals, through the Psalmist, that this treachery would be carried out, not by a stranger, but by someone close to Jesus:

"Even my bosom friend in whom I trusted, who ate of my bread, has lifted his heel against me."
(Psalm 41:9)

Jesus had full knowledge of who this would be. Therefore that which was spoken of, hundreds of years before, by David, was referred to, in John 13:10,11 & 18, by the Lord at the Last Supper, on the very night He was betrayed.

(e) The Pain Of His Death: There are many prophetic references that reveal the different aspects of the agonizing death Jesus would die: Psalm 22:1, 6 & 7, 14-18. Psalm 69:21, Isaiah 50:6 and Isaiah 53:1-10. These underline the point that His death was neither, an unexpected abrupt end to a good life, brought about by the will of man, nor a sincere attempt by Jesus to help others that had disastrously gone wrong. Rather, as the prophet says,

"It was the will of the Lord to bruise Him; He has put Him to grief...." (Isaiah 53:10a)

Everything taking place was under God's control and part of His carefully orchestrated plan.

(f) **The Promise Of His Resurrection:** What is remarkable is that Jesus Himself spoke of His own resurrection. When He came to Jerusalem with His disciples He took them aside and said,

> "... the Son of man will be delivered to the chief priests and scribes, and they will condemn Him to death, and deliver Him to the Gentiles to be mocked and scourged and crucified, and He will be raised on the third day." (Matthew 20:18 & 19)

This prediction of His resurrection was something He made on several occasions, (Mark 8:31, 9:31,10:32-34, & Matthew 12:40). Furthermore, He stated to the religious leaders and the Jews who were listening to His teaching,

> "No one takes my life from me, but I have power to lay it down of my own accord. I have power to lay it down, and I have power to take it again..."
> (John 10:18)

The Future Belongs To God

Why should we worry about the future when we see that God is in control? The unknown, though, has always held both a fear and fascination for mankind. Today 6 out of every 10 adults in this country read their horoscopes regularly because they want to know how things are going to 'pan out' for them. In universities there are professors of Futurology, whose job it is to give lectures on what will happen in the coming years. Throughout industry there are 'Think Tanks', experts who get together to try and predict how soon the world will run out of metals, oil, coal and other natural resources. Therefore, we have people going from Old Moore's Almanac to scientific predictions, desperately trying to find out about the future.

When we believe God truly is Lord there is no need to ever be fearful about what lies ahead. Being confident about His sovereign ability gives us good reason to rest secure because we know we are safe in His purpose. We can remain secure by choosing to believe the future belongs to God and rests firmly in His hands.

The Bible has got the best record of predictions being fulfilled over any other book that has ever been published. More than a quarter of the Bible contains prophecies about the future. Altogether something like 737 historical events were predicted in the Bible before they ever took place. Some of them are made once, others up to 300 times. The wonderful thing is that 594 of those predictions have already come to pass! – 82% have already been fulfilled to the letter! The reason why it is only 82% is because the remainder are to do with the end of the world and the return of Jesus Christ.

Every one of the prophecies that foretold the first coming of Jesus have been fulfilled precisely; therefore, we can be confident and sure that what is spoken regarding His second coming will also come to pass. In fact the same writers, who hundreds of years before the event predicted the first coming of Christ, are the same writers who proclaim His return as King of Kings and Lord of Lords!

In conclusion: the eternal God is still, very much, on the throne and His plan for you and purpose for the Church is to unite all things in Christ. Our part is, to choose to rest secure in His sovereignty, and work confidently to have a life that reveals, to the principalities and powers, the manifold wisdom and grace of God. This we can do with the assurance, that even when **(a) Deception Sidetracks The Proud, (b) Difficulty Strikes The Faithful,** and **(c) Demonic Forces Oppose The Anointed,** God's great purposes still are being accomplished and our destiny will be fulfilled!

Chapter 3

Choosing To Develop Divine Dimensions

No, this is not a chapter about how to have a bulging, muscular physique like Arnold Schwarzenegger, or an eye-catching figure like Kate Moss, impressive and desirable though that might be to some. What we are considering here is increasing the spiritual dimensions of our lives that determine our capacity to receive from God. In doing so we can make sure we are not restricted in reaching our destiny. This requires a choice, but by making that decision we will be more productive, effective and content in God's calling. Without progressive development we experience discouragement because our lives remain ordinary and achieve very little for the Lord.

Whether it is growth in our character, ministry, faith, confidence, compassion or evangelism etc., the key to every aspect of development is prayer. Fulfilling our destiny is impossible without the decision first to make prayer the major priority of our daily discipline. An individual can go no further than the extent to which they are prepared to sacrifice themselves in prayer. When that choice is made, though, the Bible says,

> "... The earnest (*heartfelt, continued*) prayer of a righteous man makes tremendous power available - dynamic in its working."   (James 5:16b, Amp.)

Spiritual development is inseparably linked to the depth of our prayer life; it is the primary way in which we express our dependence on God and draw from His strength. Therefore, the goal of our development should be that, from out of our relationship and right standing with Him, our prayers are earnest, heartfelt and continued. In turn, He will make such dynamic power available that when we pray for the sick they will be healed. As we pray against demonic oppression, demons will be cast out. In praying for guidance we will receive a clear sense of God's direction is for each situation.

The Prayer Of Jabez

Curiously, Jabez is remembered not for what he did but for what he prayed. His prayer became the casting distinction in his life. We read of this man in 1 Chronicles 4:9 & 10 and the lessons that can be learned from him go a long way in helping us develop into all that the Lord has destined us to be:

"Jabez was more honourable than his brothers; and his mother called his name Jabez, saying, 'because I bore him in pain.' Jabez called on the God of Israel, saying, 'Oh that thou wouldst bless me and enlarge my borders, and that thy hand might be with me, and that thou wouldst keep me from harm so that it might not hurt me!' And God granted what he asked."

Before looking at the main substance of his prayer, let us observe from these two simple verses four very encouraging things:

(a) The Magnificent Can Be Found In The Mundane: These wonderful words of Jabez emerge right in the middle of what appears to be a very monotonous and uninteresting situation. Looking at the verses that surround them, the chapters that precede them and those that immediately follow; we find just a lot of names that are hard to pronounce and seem to say very little. Unless you are a 'genealogy buff' they appear about as interesting as watching paint dry! However, right in the middle of this seemingly dull and difficult passage, listing the genealogy of the Southern Kingdom of Judah, we find these two magnificent verses among the *"begats"* and *"begots."*

Such a discovery teaches us that the most exciting things can be found in the most improbable places. That's the wonder of the Bible; we can discover something that can feed, enrich and strengthen our lives, even when looking at what might appear to be quite mundane.

(b) Nobody Is Ever Insignificant To God: Here we have the only occasion in scripture that the person, Jabez, is mentioned; nothing more is known about him, he is just one obscure name amongst a multitude of other names.

This little-known individual appears very ordinary and unimportant, yet suddenly he lights up the passage and brings it alive, shining like a beam of light in a dark and desolate place. Though he only makes this single appearance in the Bible, he leaves his mark on history and, in doing so, reminds us of the difference one life can make. This solitary occasion on which he appears in scripture, has spoken volumes to people over the centuries, so that millions of others have been able to benefit.

We should never think of ourselves as insignificant and unable to make much of a difference; the heart response we make to God not only affects us, but also others for years to come. Our names can resonate throughout history and the story we leave behind can inspire the lives of many.

(c) **Our Future Is Not Determined By Our Past:** It was the faith of Jabez that triumphed over his name. The meaning of his name, which was given to him by his mother, literally translated from the Hebrew means, *"He gives pain,"* or as the Amplified Bible says, *"sorrow maker."* What a label to carry around from birth! It's one thing occasionally being called 'a pain in the neck' by someone, even in a light-hearted way, but if right from your earliest memory you were consistently reminded of the pain you brought, it could easily become like a curse upon your life. If someone says something often enough to us we can gradually start to believe it.

The names given to people in Bible times were extremely important; unlike the way we tend to choose names for children in our culture today. More often than not, people decide on names that are to do with fashion or because they remember someone who left an impression on them. In the Bible, though, the name given to a child spoke of their future character and had a prophetic aspect to it, referring to what the child would become. For example, Jacob means 'supplanter' or 'one who tricks' - he cheated his brother out of his birthright (Genesis 27:36). Jeremiah means, 'exalted of God' - he was raised up as a prophet to speak to a nation of self-righteous people. Abraham's name means, 'father of a great multitude'

(Genesis 17:5). And of course the name Jesus prophetically meant, 'God saves.' (Matthew 1:21)

Therefore, for Jabez, his name was certainly not much of an encouragement to seeing his destiny fulfilled; in fact it was a considerable handicap. When we think of this man, though, what we learn is that our future is not determined by our past, nor dictated by man, but by our response to God.

(d) God Delights To Answer Prayer: Verse 10 concludes by saying, *"And God granted what he asked."* The result of this man deciding to seek God rather than being discouraged or feeling sorry for himself was that the Lord responded to him and honoured his faith. In every difficult circumstance of life we have the choice to call out to God or to turn away from Him to other sources of help. Throughout the Bible we are consistently reminded that the Lord delights to answer our prayers; if we are to realise our destiny we need to be convinced of this, beyond any shadow of doubt. There is never any reluctance in God's heart to grant us His blessing:

"Call unto me, and I will answer thee, and show thee great and mighty things, which thou knowest not." (Jeremiah 33:3, AV)

"... anyone who comes to Him must believe that He exists and that He rewards those who earnestly seek Him." (Hebrews 11:6, NIV)

"What man of you, if his son ask him for bread, will give him a stone? Or if he asks for a fish, will give him a serpent? If you then, who are evil, know how to give good gifts to your children, how much more will your Father who is in heaven give good things to those who ask Him!" (Matthew 7:9-11)

As we come now to the main substance in the prayer of Jabez, let us consider four aspects of his heartfelt petition to God. In doing so we gain some insight into what enabled him to develop the dimensions of his life and fulfil his destiny:

Firstly, Praying For The Blessing Of God

As far as Jabez was concerned, the most important desire he had was expressed as he cried out, *"Oh that thou wouldst bless me...."* He called upon the only one who could and who would make the difference in his life. There is a direct correlation between living in God's blessing and achieving God's purpose. He doesn't bless us that we might boast of what *we've* accomplished, or received; His blessings are to equip us to accomplish His purpose and the destiny He has planned for our lives.

The use of the word 'blessing', in our own vocabulary and thinking, has such a shallow meaning. If someone happens to sneeze we automatically say, "Bless you", or if we thank a person for something they've done for us we might use the same expression. Even in praying we can ask God to bless the missionaries of the world, bless our children and to bless our food, without fully appreciating what we are saying. What is meant in the Bible though has a far deeper intention than many may understand.

The word "bless" in the Old Testament means, *"to endue with power for success, prosperity, health etc."* Blessed comes from the Hebrew word "Barak", meaning *"to invoke divine favour upon, to bring the benefits of God upon, or to cause to prosper."* In asking God to bless us, or when we desire to bless someone else, we should do so with the expectancy that something will actually be imparted - not merely words, but spiritual resources and power!

At some point, Jabez recognised the need for God to work mightily in his life, that he might receive what he could not gain on his own. When we pray, *"Oh that you would bless me,"* we are asking that God would give to us a spiritual impartation to meet a particular need: His anointing, wisdom, effectiveness, guidance etc. – that which is necessary for us to continue walking in victory and to fulfil our destiny. It means asking for the unlimited and unfathomable riches of God's goodness to be laid upon our lives. We should never settle for a mediocre Christian life and never be satisfied with where we are spiritually because there is so much more for us to move into and experience.

Therefore, while it is true that we have already been *"blessed with every spiritual blessing in heavenly places"* (Ephesians 1:3b),

we still need to continually appropriate this in our daily life and present circumstances. Jesus emphasised our responsibility to come before God, on the basis of our relationship with Him as our heavenly Father, and ask for what we recognise we are lacking. He taught His disciples,
> *"Ask, and it will be given you; seek, and you will find; knock and it will be opened to you."*   (Luke 11:9)

Before we can effectively pray this aspect of the prayer and expect to receive something further that will enrich our lives, certain steps are essential:

(a) **A Transformation Of Thinking:** To fulfil our destiny we must get away from 'small mindedness'; the feeling that to dare to pray such a prayer is an 'unspiritual' or a selfish thing to be asking. While the prayer of Jabez was personal, it was not selfish. By looking at this man we see that he was not a self-centred individual because the Bible tells us he was, *"more honourable than his brothers."* (verse 9). He was a man of integrity and a man of prayer. When God looked at his heart He could see an honourable man, who with faith was seeking after Him, which is why his request was granted. What others think, or how they might interpret our desire for the fullness of God's blessing, is unimportant; the only thing that really matters is the Lord's evaluation as He searches our hearts.

We are no use for God's purposes and powerless to help other people unless we first know that the fullness of God's blessing is upon our lives. When Peter and John were coming to pray at the temple one day, they met someone in deep need. He had been lame from birth and was begging for material help. Peter confidently said to him, *"...Look at us."* (Acts 3:4b). This, I know, is quite disturbing to the merely religious who immediately take offence and say that people should not look at '*us*' they must look at Jesus! Such an objection is extremely naive because a true Christian is the clearest example of what Jesus is actually like. If people cannot see Christ in our lives then they are unlikely to do so anywhere else.

Having directed the lame man's gaze upon himself Peter then says,
> *"Silver and gold have I none; but such as I have give I thee: in the name of Jesus Christ of Nazareth rise up and walk."* (verse 6, AV)

As Peter imparted the blessing of God to him, it resulted not only in the healing of the man. Also it brought a great challenge to the religious leaders, as well as a powerful witness to everyone else looking on, concluding in the conversion of over 5,000 people! Notice though, Peter said, *"Such as I have give I thee...."* Peter couldn't give what he hadn't got, but because he was living in the fullness of God's blessing he had a tremendous amount to give! Our cry for greater blessing is in order that we might be rich in God's resources and therefore in a position where we can be a blessing and help to others. We can achieve nothing of any eternal value without the confidence that our life is 'blessed' by God.

(b) **A Sacrificial Offering:** The willingness of the Lord to bless is seen in the challenge He made, through the prophet Malachi, for His people to prove His promise for themselves:
> *"Bring the full tithes into the storehouse, that there may be food in my house; and thereby put me to the test, says the Lord of hosts, if I will not open the windows of heaven for you and pour down for you an overflowing blessing."* (Malachi 3:10)

God's eagerness to pour down this promised blessing is spoken of in the context of His people honouring Him by bringing acceptable sacrifices and offerings. Those referred to in Malachi were robbing God. He had already made clear that the sacrifice His people should bring needed to be pure and spotless. Every animal brought to Him as an offering had to be the best, yet His people were trying to get away with offering animals that were blind and lame, thinking that God would not notice. Furthermore, some of them weren't giving the full amount they were commanded to in their tithes. Even so, God guaranteed, that if they would bring what they owed, He would pour out a tremendous blessing upon them that would be far greater than that which they had given.

The same is true today; if we are to walk in His blessing we have to honour Him, not in sacrificing animals, but in tithing (giving a tenth part of our finances) and in the offering of our lives, so that we give our best when making any sacrifice to Him. Those who object to tithing, on the grounds that they are no longer under law but living under grace, always do so with the aim of giving less rather than more than a tenth of their finances. However, should we give less now that we are under grace than we did when we were under the law? It is impossible to fulfil our destiny if we are robbing God; He is no man's debtor, which is why Jesus taught,

> *"Give, and it shall be given to you, good measure, pressed down, shaken together, running over, will be put into your lap. For the measure you give will be the measure you get back."*   (Luke 6:38)

Obedience always secures the blessing of God. This was emphasised when the Lord, speaking to His people through Moses, made a clear promise of His willingness to bless every aspect of their lives, on the condition that they would walk in obedience to His Word:

> *"And if you obey the voice of the Lord your God, being careful to do all His commandments... The Lord will command the blessing upon you in your barns, and in all that you undertake..."*
> (Deuteronomy 28:1 & 8)

(c) **A Single Minded Determination:** The account of Jacob wrestling with God until daybreak is an illustration teaching us the importance of having determination and tenacity to lay hold of the blessing of the Lord. Jacob said, *"...I will not let you go, unless you bless me."* (Genesis 32:26b). This is the attitude that attracts a spiritual impartation; not merely a belief that God is *able* to bless, but a conviction and persistency of faith that knows He *will*, if we refuse to let go of His promise to do so. The assurance of God's willingness to bless causes us to hold on, travailing in prayer, until we know we have received what is necessary to fulfil our destiny.

In 2 Kings 2, we read of Elisha walking together with Elijah, who was coming towards the end of his great and powerful ministry. Elisha had seen the difference God's blessing had made in his mentor's life through outstanding miracles and supernatural demonstrations of God's power. Now he had a longing to fulfil his own destiny and not simply to live in the background of someone else's.

He determined to stay with Elijah like a shadow, not letting him out of his sight, even though Elijah kept saying to him, *"Tarry here, I pray you; for the Lord has sent me to…."* (verses 2, 4, & 6). As Elisha continued to walk closely with him Elijah said, *"Ask what I shall do for you, before I am taken from you"* (verse 9). His reply was to ask Elijah not merely for a blessing, but he said, *"... let me inherit a double share of your spirit."* (verse 9b). He wanted to develop and see his own sphere of ministry grow, so he sought a double portion of the same anointing and spirit that was upon the one he admired so much.

Elijah responded by making him the promise that if he would fix his eyes upon him and watch his departure when he was taken up into heaven, then he would receive what he was seeking. Having been given such a promise, Elisha had an expectancy and determination that nothing could distract; he kept his eyes firmly fixed on the man of God. When the moment came, and Elijah was suddenly taken up into heaven, the mantle that had been upon Elijah fell to Elisha and he received what he knew would help him fulfil God's purpose for his life.

(d) **A Maintaining Of Unity:** One other example of God's condition and willingness to bless is found in the words of David. He says in Psalm 133:1 & 3b,
"Behold, how good and how pleasant it is when brothers dwell in unity! …. For there the Lord has commanded the blessing…."

When God commands His blessing, no person on earth or demon from hell can block it. This will only be sent though, where there is unity; when there are right attitudes and right relationships between God's people. The blessing of God will rarely come upon an individual or a church where there is known discord resulting from issues that haven't been put right.

It is for this reason that we must take great care to maintain the unity of the Spirit. Any resentment, bitterness or wrong attitudes, particularly towards a fellow believer, will not only quench the Holy Spirit but also rob us of the blessing of God. The Bible takes this very seriously, which is why forgiveness is such a major key to living in victory. It was Mahatma Gandhi who stated, "An eye for an eye makes the whole world blind." Wrong attitudes will always hinder our destiny. Therefore, Jesus taught,

> "Love your enemies, do good to those who hate you, bless those who curse you, pray for those who abuse you." (Luke 6:28)

Furthermore, Paul writing to the Christians in Rome said,
> "If possible, so far as it depends upon you, live peaceably with all." (Romans 12:18)

From the examples we have considered, it is evident that far more is involved than just asking to be blessed. When we fulfil the conditions of God's Word we place ourselves under an 'Open Heaven' and are in a position to receive the divine impartation that we seek.

Secondly, Praying For Our Borders To Be Enlarged

Having asked, *"Oh that thou wouldst bless me..."* Jabez then goes on to voice the second aspect of his petition, *"... and enlarge my borders...."* Such a prayer expresses the desire for greater influence and responsibility, for further possibilities to be more and do more for God. The Lord is able to open doors of opportunity and bring people across our path so that our effectiveness is increased, but we need to yearn for our borders to be enlarged. Just like Caleb, who at 85 years of age was still crying out, *"...give me this mountain..."* (Joshua 14:12, AV), our request to the Lord needs to indicate that we are not 'settling down,' but are determined to reach out beyond our present limitations.

If we are to live in God's blessing and move into all He has prepared for us to do, we must make a choice to personally change, so that what we are and where we are at any given moment is consistent with the destiny He has for us.

While reading the excellent daily reading notes, 'Word For Today', I came across this fascinating illustration written by Bob Gass: Alfred Nobel was a Swedish chemist who made his fortune by inventing dynamite and other explosives used for weapons. When his brother died, a newspaper printed Alfred's obituary by mistake. It described him as a man who'd become rich by enabling people to kill each other in unprecedented numbers. Deeply shaken, he resolved to use his fortune to reward accomplishments that benefited humanity – hence The Nobel Prize. Nobel had the rare opportunity to re-evaluate his life towards the end and still live long enough to change and do something about it.

Comedian, Jerry Lewis, joked that the best wedding gift given to him was a film of the entire marriage ceremony. He said that when things got really bad at home, he'd go into a room, close the door, run the film backwards and walk out a free man! We probably will never be able to do that, or read our own obituary in the newspaper, but we can, however, make a personal choice to alter what we alone can change, while we have the opportunity.

Change must always start on an individual level and is an integral part of any personal destiny being fulfilled. The words inscribed on the tomb of an Anglican Bishop in Westminster Abbey bear out the importance of this:

> "In my youth, my imagination had no limits. I dreamed of changing the world. But as I grew older and wiser, I found that the world would not change, so I decided to change my country. But it, too, seemed immovable. So as I grew in my twilight years, in one last attempt, I settled for changing my family; but alas they would have none of it. Now on my deathbed I realise that if I had first changed myself, then by example, I might have changed my family, and through my family changed the world."

God, as our Creator and Father, is committed to bringing change into our lives that will result in our development. While we might think this cannot be imposed upon us the Lord nevertheless, in His great love and divine purpose will accomplish it, even when we might not like the way He decides to do so. He will prune away anything that chokes the new life lying latent within, so that our potential will blossom. Letting the Lord cut back even that which appears to be good and fruitful, is the only way to see our destiny fully realised. Jesus taught His disciples,

> *"Every branch of mine that bears no fruit, He takes away, and every branch that does bear fruit He prunes, that it may bear more fruit."* (John 15:2)

For each believer there are borders around their lives that need changing, things that are restricting them from developing and moving beyond where they are at the moment. In some cases these have been placed there by themselves, or perhaps due to circumstances, the opinions of other people, or by the devil. We must refuse to accept any borders that inhibit our development and restrict our faith, ministry, confidence, liberty, and effectiveness. Anything God has not placed around our lives can only work against the destiny He has for us.

The borders restricting us may be things like fear, doubt, sickness, failure, discouragement or sinful habits. Whatever they are, they all have the same effect of holding us back. Therefore, the constant prayer of our heart needs to be, *"Lord enlarge my borders."*

(a) **Self-Imposed Borders:** There is a natural tendency within us all to settle for the mediocre. While we ought to be pressing on and seeing every possibility realised, we impose upon ourselves restrictions that are dictated more by our low expectations, self-consciousness and fears than the Word of God. We were never destined to be just average. In the beginning, when God looked at His creation, the greatest of which was mankind, the Bible tells us He looked and saw that it was *"very good."* (Genesis 1:31). Average doesn't look so good when you realise that it's just the worst of the best and the best of the worst! At the end of the day, dying with commitments undefined, convictions undeclared, service unfulfilled and dreams unrealised is one of the saddest things of all.

Each one of us is capable of so much more than we can possibly imagine. It was forty-eight years ago that Johnny Weismuller, the greatest swimmer in the world at that time, held fifty world records. Today, thirteen-year-old girls break his achievements every time they go into the pool. We shouldn't restrict ourselves by settling for what appears to be our 'limit'. The frontiers of achievement are there for us to discover, break through and move beyond.

(b) **Personal Circumstances:** Abraham Lincoln said, "Success is going from failure to failure without losing your enthusiasm". How easy it is to allow difficult personal circumstances to dampen our enthusiasm and take the fire out of our motivation. Self-pity, resulting from hardship, will cause us to be bound by our circumstances. In reality, though, there is no situation, regardless of how painful or impossible it might appear, that should ever restrict us from discovering the greatness of our destiny.

Every person who has ever accomplished anything worthwhile, faced difficulty and possible defeat, but refused to give in: John Bunyan wrote Pilgrims Progress from prison; Florence Nightingale, too ill to move from her bed, reorganised the hospitals of England; Louis Pasteur, the greatest biologist of the 19th century became semi-paralysed by apoplexy, but was tireless in his attack on disease; American historian, Francis Parkman was unable to work for more than five minutes at a time - his eyesight was so bad that he could only scrawl gigantic words on a manuscript - yet he wrote twenty magnificent volumes of history. Great accomplishment comes through the process of overcoming grim adversity.

(c) **People's Opinion:** If only Christians took more notice of what God had to say, rather than the opinions of others, they'd discover their hidden greatness. It is so true that *"Death and life are in the power of the tongue."* (Proverbs 18:21a). All too often, we listen to what others say about what is and isn't possible, and their negativity brings a deadness into our inventiveness and dreams. Whenever God speaks, though, His Word breathes life because it is *"living and active"* (Hebrews 4:12). There is creativity and power in what He says. Therefore, if our destiny is to be achieved, it will only be as we are prepared to disregard every opinion of man that contradicts what we know the Lord has said to us. This doesn't of course mean that we are not mindful for the need of godly council, but mere opinions in themselves we can do without. We learn from history that those who disregarded opinions based simply on logic always enlarged the borders of what was considered possible. Even the opinions of eminent men can be seriously flawed:

Dr. Dionysus Lardner, of London University said in 1830, "Rail travel at high speed is not possible because passengers, unable to breathe, would die of asphyxiation."

In 1876, American President, Rutherford Hayes was quoted as saying, "This telephone is an amazing invention, but who would ever want to use one of them?"

A British Parliamentary Committee, in 1878, set up to investigate electric lighting, said of Edison's electric light bulb, "It is good enough for our transatlantic friends, but unworthy of the attentions of practical or scientific men."

A Bank President, advising against investing in Ford Motors, said in 1903, "The horse is here to stay, but the automobile is only a novelty, a passing fad." - How wrong and inhibiting man's opinions can be!

To see the borders around our lives enlarged, it is not sufficient just to pray and express our desire to God, or even to be willing to change. We also need to take personal steps of faith ourselves. In the case of Joshua's destiny, God intended to enlarge the borders around his life and ministry and gave him a glimpse of this when He said, *"Every place that the sole of your foot will tread upon I have given to you..."* (Joshua 1:3). While the promise was encouraging, and must have stirred a strong motivation within him, he had to be the one who would take those steps and actually move forward.

This aspect of what we must do, in co-operation with God's promise, was emphasised by the Lord when He said, through the prophet Isaiah,

> *"Enlarge the place of your tent, and let the curtains of your habitations be stretched out; hold not back, lengthen your cords and strengthen your stakes. For you will spread abroad to the right and to the left...."*
> (Isaiah 54:2 & 3)

Here, God's Word is speaking of our need to make plans in readiness for the expansion and development that He wants to bring about. It implies preparation, expectancy and effort to make sure those borders restricting us are pushed back. To do something that expresses faith might for some simply mean: speaking out publicly in prayer for the first time; going to minister to someone that is sick; finding a person to witness to; moving out in the gifts of the Holy Spirit; beginning to dance, raising our hands or kneeling before God in worship. The point is that, if we are to develop, we must choose to move beyond where we are at the moment, and do whatever it is that we have never done before.

It has been said that, the difference between the ordinary and the extraordinary is the willingness to do the "extra". We must choose to do the "extra" to bring about the extraordinary work of God in our own lives.

Thirdly,
Praying For The Assurance Of God's Presence

The third aspect of Jabez's prayer was, *"...and that your hand might be with me."* God's hand being with a person guarantees, among other things, an assurance of spiritual authority and power, victory, favour and direction. It results in a quiet confidence that is expressed through knowing His abiding presence in everyday life. While the Lord intends every believer to move out in faith and into all that His Word promises, He doesn't expect them to do this alone, and certainly not in their own strength, but under His anointing.

When Moses was called to go to Pharaoh and bring deliverance to God's people, he was extremely anxious about his ability to carry out the task. Having made several excuses and offered good, rational reasons why he couldn't do what was being expected of him, he eventually yielded to God's will and reluctantly agreed to take on the job. Before he would go though, he wanted the assurance that God's presence would be with him (Exodus 3:11 & 12). This request continued to be a need in his life, especially when being conscious of the burden of his responsibility:

"*If thy presence will not go with me, do not carry us up from here.*" (Exodus 33:15)

Joshua was in need of this same assurance when taking over from Moses because, although he had watched and helped this great leader in the past, he personally had never had the scale of responsibility that was now before him. To be able, not only to confidently move forward himself, but also lead others into greater blessing, he needed to know that the Lord was with him. God was calling him, just as He had called Moses years earlier, to broaden his borders and to move into a larger ministry. So, to make this possible, He gave to Joshua the promise of His presence:

"*…. as I was with Moses, so I will be with you; I will not fail you or forsake you.*" (Joshua 1:5b)

This is necessary in our own lives before we can move boldly into what God is calling us to. We need the reminder that the God of Moses, the disciples, the apostle Paul and all the great 'giants of faith' throughout church history, is our God, and will be with us just as powerfully, if we simply trust Him. The reassuring promises He gave to them still apply to us today. This is why, when Jesus commissioned His disciples to go and preach the gospel, against severe opposition, He said to them,

"*… and lo, I am with you always, even to the close of the age.*" (Matthew 28:20b)

As the disciples took God at His Word and in obedience moved confidently forward, the dimensions of their expectation, effectiveness and experience were enlarged because the presence of the Lord was right alongside them in everything they did:

"*… the Lord worked with them and confirmed the message by the signs that attended it.*" (Mark 16:20)

There are distinctive characteristics that immediately set a person apart from all others, when they have the assurance of God's hand being with them:

(a) Spiritual Authority And Power: The hallmark, most evident throughout the New Testament, of true authority and power was signs and wonders which confirmed the word of those who preached the gospel. God's presence, working alongside His people, was seen in remarkable miracles that in turn produced effective evangelism.

Try as we may, with all our planning, clever ideas and latest technology, fruitfulness in evangelism falls flat without the supernatural. All our time, energy and resources cannot produce any substitute more effective, to arrest the attention and hold the interest of unconverted people, than the presence of God performing miracles. In the book of Acts we find ordinary, uneducated disciples doing extraordinary works. They saw the most amazing impact being made as they preached, because God's hand was with them:

"And now, Lord, look upon their threats, and grant to thy servants to speak thy word with all boldness, while thou stretchest out thy hand to heal, and signs and wonders are performed through the name of thy holy servant Jesus." (Acts 4:29)

This same impact is seen in Antioch where the disciples were, for the first time, called Christians. It was the hand of God that brought to the people conviction of sin and a sense of their spiritual need:

"And the hand of the Lord was with them, and a great number that believed turned to the Lord."
(Acts 11:21)

(b) Victory Over Our Enemies: Opposition to the gospel was certainly expected in the New Testament; in fact, to be a Christian then was extremely costly because committed believers in Christ immediately attracted enemies. To preach Christ and live by His Word always provokes a reaction from others, particularly the religious and the

rebellious, just as it did in the early Church. Paul made clear what should be expected when he said,
> "Indeed all who desire to live a godly life in Christ Jesus will be persecuted." (2 Timothy 3:12)

Whether our enemies are spiritual or otherwise, ultimately Satan who is seeking to resist God's purpose influences them. Whatever the devil and all his demons may try to do though, and however he tries to bring restriction into our lives, his influence is broken when God's hand is with us. Moses understood this which is why he said,
> "Thy right hand, O Lord, glorious in power, shatters the enemy. In the greatness of thy majesty thou overthrowest thy adversaries." (Exodus 15:6)

(c) **Respect Given And Favour Found:** Though some may ridicule our faith and mock our commitment to Christ, the presence of God's blessing will eventually cause them to respect what they see:
> "When a man's ways please the Lord, He makes even his enemies to be at peace with him." (Proverbs 16:7)

This was the case for the first Christians. Although they often received strong opposition there were times when they found themselves,
> "... having favour with all the people." (Acts 2:47)

Also occasions when,
> "... the people held them in high honour." (Acts 5:13)

Ultimately, people will begin to respect the testimony for which we stand as we maintain a righteous attitude towards them. This is why the Bible says,
> "Humble yourselves under the mighty hand of God, that in due time He may exalt you." (1 Peter 5:6)

We don't have to justify what we do, apologise for what we believe, or push ourselves forward. Nor do we need to worry about other people's approval or acceptance of us, because our destiny is in the mighty hand of God, who will, in due time, exalt us.

While preaching in the centre of Leicester on one occasion, we had an extremely vicious heckler verbally attacking what was being said. He confronted us, full of anger and hatred toward the gospel; at the top of his voice he began berating and abusing us in a very threatening way. As he was waving his fists and shouting obscenities, an unconverted lady, who wasn't even a 'church goer', passed by and stopped to listen. After a short while she rebuked the man, telling him to have some respect, to keep quiet and leave us alone. He refused to take any notice of her and just carried on ranting, so the woman jumped on him and hit him with her handbag! Stunned by this, the man, who was so full of bravado and threats was immediately silenced. He scuttled away in seconds as this non-Christian lady respected and defended our witness!

(d) **Direction And Guidance:** If we are to live in the good of all God has prepared for us, we need to know that His hand is upon our lives to lead and guide each step we take. That which the Lord did as He led Israel out of the bondage of Egypt, through the wilderness for forty years, and into the Promised Land, He is able to do for all His children. We can't expect to fulfil our destiny if we are unsure of the direction in which our lives should be heading. Knowing God's will and walking in the centre of His purpose must be something we seek as a priority.

What never ceases to amaze me is the number of Christians that stumble on unaware of any definite direction. They lurch from one crisis to the next and walk in a fog of uncertainty concerning God's will. His promise, though, could not be clearer:

"Your ears shall hear a word behind you, saying, 'This is the way, walk in it,' when you turn to the right or when you turn to the left." (Isaiah 30:21)

The prophet Ezekiel is a good example of someone who knew God's direction throughout his ministry. That guidance was expressed in his writings with the key phrase,

"The hand of the Lord was upon me...."
(Ezekiel 3:14b & 22, also 37:1 & 40:1b)

Fourthly, Praying For God's Divine Protection

The last aspect of this unique prayer of Jabez is to do with accepting that while we are in the 'hollow of God's hand,' His protection does not necessarily mean we won't ever face times of hardship and temptation. Jabez prayed,
   *"... that thou wouldst keep me from harm **so that it might not hurt me!**"*

As God's hand of blessing is upon us and as our borders are enlarged, so we might move out into all we have been called to be, inevitably there will come difficulties and setbacks. Problems will beset our ministry, our well-being, and the welfare of our family. These have the potential of shaking our faith, obscuring our vision, sidetracking our direction, and preventing us realising our destiny.

The prayer here of Jabez, then, is not that we should be kept from the pressures and difficulties of life - immune from any trials and testing around. Just looking at the history of God's people Israel, Jesus Himself, the Church generally and those believers who have suffered and died for their faith, demonstrates this is not likely. However, we can pray with Jabez, *"...that it might not hurt me."* With such a request, what we are asking is that the Attraction of sin, Adverse circumstances of life, Assassination attempts by man and the Attack of Satan, will not ultimately have a damaging effect, hurting our God-given destiny.

   (a)   **The Attraction Of Sin:** We must constantly be alert, if we are to be kept from the alluring pitfalls that are in the world, so we can be guided away from that which could do us great harm. This is consistent with what Jesus taught His disciples when He said they were to pray, *".... lead us not into temptation, but deliver us from evil."* (Matthew 6:13). God requires us to learn more than just how to resist temptation, but also to stay away from its attraction, which is why His Word says, *"Avoid every kind of evil."* (1 Thessalonians 5:22, NIV). He has given us both the ability to say "no" to sin, and the wisdom to distance ourselves from the things that might cause us harm. It is a personal choice.

With all spiritual development come opportunities for failure. The history of the Church is strewn with the wreckage of Christians who have fallen into sin, and left their destiny, all because they allowed themselves to be drawn too close to the flame of temptation. The more God blesses and uses a person, the more they need to be prepared for spiritual conflicts, as they become Satan's target for deception. Through temptation any believer can so easily be seduced, persuaded or allured into evil. Lutheran Pastor and theologian Dietrich Bonhoeffer writing about man's vulnerability to the attraction of sin said:

> "In our members there is a slumbering inclination towards desire which is both sudden and fierce. With irresistible power desire seizes mastery over the flesh. All at once a secret, smouldering fire is kindled. The flesh burns and is in flames. It makes no difference whether it is sexual desire or ambition or vanity or desire for revenge or love of fame and power or greed for money."

At times, when we find ourselves in unsafe places, the wisest thing we can do is make a swift exit:
"And He said to man, 'Behold, the fear of the Lord, that is wisdom; and to depart from evil is understanding." (Job 28:28)

This was something Joseph chose to do when Potiphar's wife tempted him. As she tried to seduce him he didn't linger, rather he immediately fled from her (Genesis 39:7-12). In fulfilling our destiny this choice is clearly presented in God's Word:
"The highway of the upright turns aside from evil; he who guards his way preserves his life."
(Proverbs 16:17)

Safe living is sometimes found in quick departures, as is seen in Paul's charge to his young disciple Timothy:

> *"But you, man of God, flee from all this, and pursue righteousness, godliness, faith, love, endurance and gentleness."* (1 Timothy 6:11, NIV)

(b) **The Adverse Circumstances Of Life:** We'll be looking at adversity in greater depth when we come to Chapter 8, but what is worth noting here is that, although all sorts of dangers and difficulties may confront us, they need not damage our destiny. This is because, as we considered previously, when we believe in the sovereignty of God we can have confidence that, *"... in everything God works for good..."* (Romans 8:28). Ultimately, whatever we go through can in the long term, never hurt us, which is why God said to the prophet Isaiah,

> *"When you pass through the waters I will be with you; and through the rivers, they shall not overwhelm you; when you walk through the fire you shall not be burned, and the flame shall not consume you."* (Isaiah 43:2)

The spiritual dimensions of our lives can be developed, rather than destroyed, through experiences of pain, which is why David said, *"... thou hast enlarged me when I was in distress...."* (Psalm 4:1, AV). This is only possible though when we have a godly attitude towards what we are experiencing. In maintaining a right spirit we can grow and be strengthened through trials as James explains:

> *"Count it all joy, my brethren, when you meet various trials, for you know that the testing of your faith produces steadfastness. And let steadfastness have its full effect, that you may be perfect and complete, lacking nothing* (James 1:2-4)

(c) **The Assassination Attempts Against Our Character:** Along the road to success and development, one of the many dangers is the attempt of character assassination that people will make against us. False accusations, innuendoes, half-truths and blatant lies, all designed to undermine our integrity and destiny, are things that need to be faced with confidence. This we can do, knowing we are in good company. The Bible says of Jesus,

> *"He made Himself of no reputation...."*
> (Philippians 2:7, AV)

In fact, religious leaders even accused Him of being possessed by the devil, and being motivated by evil powers. (Mark 3:22). Others, speaking against the apostle Paul, said,
> *"... your great learning is turning you mad."*
> (Acts 26:24)

Among the accusations made against myself over the years, by so called Christians, is that I've hypnotized the congregation, I'm a demon-possessed terrorist, I've pushed people over when praying for them, I've tried to hijack and take-over a meeting and that I am anti-Semitic. Ridiculous and, may I say, untrue though these things are, if it were not for God, great damage could have been caused to my ministry and destiny. Thankfully, the promise of the Lord is that intended harm shall not hurt us:
> *"No weapon that is formed against you shall prosper, and every tongue that shall rise against you in judgement you shall show to be in the wrong."* (Isaiah 54:17, Amp.)

Also, Paul's reassuring words reinforce our confidence:
> *"Who shall bring any charge against God's elect? It is God who justifies; who is to condemn?....."*
> (Romans 8:33 & 34)

(d) **The Attack Of Satan:** Working behind the scenes, in all that would seek to do us harm, is of course Satan. When looking at the demonic and vicious assault that God's enemy made against Job, it might appear that this righteous and devout servant was badly hurt. After all, his land, cattle, wealth, health, reputation, sons and daughters were ruthlessly taken from him. However, that was how things looked in the short term. What we learn, ultimately, though is that Job came through stronger, richer and doubly blessed. His borders were enlarged in every respect by the end of his ordeal, in that God gave him twice as much as he'd had before! (Job 42:10).

God allowed Satan's attack on Job for the purpose of revealing his servant's integrity (Job 1:8-11). He limited what Satan was permitted to do (verse 12). The ordeal demonstrated that the destiny of God's creation would be more glorious than the destructive intention of Satan's evil plan (Chapter 42:12-17). It also showed generations to come that the Lord's power of loving protection was greater than Satan's hatred to annihilate and separate (Romans 8:35-39).

In conclusion: maybe, like Jabez, you've had negative labels put upon you, perhaps recently, possibly many years ago; for Jabez it was right from birth. Perhaps you want to be more fruitful and develop beyond where you are, but you feel so insignificant, just one name amongst a mass of other names. Maybe you feel restricted by certain borders that are around your life, which you know have not been placed there by God. Whatever your situation, if you are determined to discover your destiny and long to develop the spiritual dimensions of your life, let your response to God be the same as that of Jabez:
"Oh that thou wouldst bless me and enlarge my borders, and that thy hand might be with me, and that thou wouldst keep me from harm so that it might not hurt me" – **And The Lord Will Grant You Your Prayer.**

Chapter 4

Choosing To Find Fulfilment In God

Over thirty-eight years ago, in 1965, rock singer Mick Jagger and the Rolling Stones sang a song that expressed a feeling of deep frustration. It carried a message that rang out around the world and was echoed in the hearts of millions of people. Immediately it became a number one record because so many could identify with its words. The title was, *"I Can't Get No Satisfaction!"*

This frustration was certainly true of life and times then, and nothing much has changed today. Despite all manner of modern conveniences that we have and the many impressive advances that have been made in technology, still dissatisfaction seems to characterize the age in which we live.

It is impossible for anyone to discover their God-given destiny until they have made a decision to find fulfilment firstly in their relationship with the Lord. This is because everything He has planned for our lives flows out of our communion and commitment to Him. God's will for us all is that we are fulfilled emotionally, physically and spiritually. We can be certain that this is so because His Word makes it very clear. David, when speaking about his discovery of fulfilment, says,

"... in thy presence is fullness of joy; at thy right hand there are pleasures for evermore." (Psalm 16:11, AV)

He was referring here to something that would last, unlike the fleeting pleasures of sin - something that had satisfied him deep within. Having found this to be a reality in his own life he then speaks from that position of certainty to help others discover the same assurance for themselves. His confident instruction affirms,

"Take delight in the Lord, and He will give you the desires of your heart." (Psalm 37:4)

The Causes Of Frustration

Before we look more closely at being fulfilled, it is necessary first for us to establish some of the major reasons why people are frustrated and live their lives thinking that, for them, satisfaction is as elusive as trying to catch hold of the wind. Even within the Church there are those who wrestle with the feeling that there must be more to their Christian lives than what they are experiencing. Such thoughts lie silently beneath the surface, often unexpressed because of the fear that others might think less of them if they knew. The reality is, though, that many other Christans feel the same way and the causes of this frustration are very common, each of which prevent people discovering their true destiny. These are:

(a) **Worldly Values:** The age in which we live is very materialistic and it is extremely hard not to get ensnared in the trap of feeling we have to *'keep up'* with what everyone around us has, otherwise we will be missing out in some way. Subtly, we can be drawn into the sub-conscious pressure of thinking that if we don't have a bigger house, better job, newer car, faster computer or the latest model of mobile phone etc. then we can't be fulfilled. The influence of being pressed into the mould of ungodly values is a very significant problem.

Whenever we begin to think firstly on a material level to find fulfilment, it will result in dissatisfaction, because no matter what we have, we will always crave for more. This is why Jesus taught,

"Where your treasure is, there will your heart be also." (Matthew 6:21)

The thing that we treasure most in life is what our hearts will be feeding on, and if we are feeding on the wrong things then we will forever be dissatisfied. It is for this reason that Jesus says, a few verses later in verse 33,

"But seek first His kingdom and His righteousness, and all these things shall be yours as well."

(b) **Unmet Emotional Needs:** Each one of us has been created with an emotional dimension to our lives. It is more evident in some than others, but every individual has emotional needs. These have got to be met, otherwise finding fulfilment will be impossible. This is why even those who have everything that money can buy, sometimes are the loneliest, saddest, most dissatisfied people you could meet. They have every material luxury meeting their physical desires, but their emotional needs are left destitute. These people soon discover, like King Solomon who lacked nothing materially, and who drank from every cup of human experience – wealth, women, and wine,

"…. *All is vanity and a striving after the wind."*
(Ecclesiastes 1:14)

The basic emotional needs we all have in common are: the need to be loved, the need to be considered a person of worth, the need to be accepted, and the need for purpose and a sense of achievement in our lives. Whenever these important areas are neglected, or we try to get them met in other people or other things, then frustration and lack of fulfilment affects us.

(c) **Confusion:** If we have no clear goals or sense of direction to our daily living, we will never discover our destiny. Instead, we will find ourselves simply going round in circles; maybe using a lot of energy and making a great deal of effort, but not getting anywhere at all. When there is a fog of uncertainty surrounding us concerning God's will and we live from day to day in an indefinite manner, then we will always be frustrated. This is because God has not only saved us from our sins and past lives, He has also set us apart to serve Him and accomplish the work He has for us to do.

The apostle Paul was conscious of this when he said in 1 Corinthians 9:26, *"I do not run aimlessly….."* He lived with a divine objective and had goals that motivated his life. He was always moving towards something specific to fulfil his destiny. Without having such clarity of purpose Paul would never have achieved the things he did. I know how true this is for example in writing. If I didn't set myself the definite objective of completing a book and have specific goals to work towards in meeting that aim, then it would never get finished. I'd be extremely frustrated because other things would take priority; time would be wasted, deadlines not met and very little would be accomplished.

(d) **Lack Of Self-Discipline:** Following on from the previous point is the need for self-discipline. We may well have a very clear objective that puts our lives on a particular path, and also well-defined goals to ensure that we arrive at our desired destination. However, without self-discipline all our dreams and aspirations will never be realised. We must not only see what God has called us to do, we also need to discipline ourselves towards that end; this is part of what it means to be a disciple. That discipline is vital in areas like our prayer life, reading and learning the scriptures, holiness of life and obedience etc. If we are not disciplined we will inevitably be frustrated. It is for this very reason Paul says in 1 Corinthians 9:25,
"*Every athlete exercises self-control in all things….*"

To win the prize and achieve what we have set out to do, a disciplined, radical lifestyle of commitment is called for. It is important to notice from this verse that no one else can do for us what is required. The trainer can only do so much for the athlete. The runner might have the best trainer in the world and when he is competing in a race he could have the encouragement and support of all in the stadium applauding his efforts and urging him to go on and win. In the final analysis though, unless he has disciplined himself, his best efforts will be frustrated and his dream unfulfilled.

(e) **An Unfruitful Life:** It is impossible for us to be fulfilled if we are living contrary to our destiny, and part of that calling is to be fruitful. Here is where a lot of people find themselves extremely frustrated. God's will for each of us is that we have a fruitful character, that we have a fruitful prayer life, and that we are fruitful in the work and

ministry He has set for us to do. The will of God for our lives in this respect, and the emphasis of our destiny, is made clear by the teaching of Jesus when He said,
> "You did not choose me, but I chose you and appointed you that you should go and bear fruit and that your fruit should abide...." (John 15:16)

If we are not bearing fruit, for whatever reason, then we are going to be frustrated.

(f) **Disappointment:** In relation to the importance of having a fruitful life, one other area that brings deep frustration is disappointment. If we have not lived up to our own aspirations, or feel we have fallen short of other people's expectations, then disappointment creeps in. Also, whenever our hopes are dashed and our dreams are shattered, or our plans have come to very little, then this will always be a barrier to our fulfilment. This might be the case perhaps where we have been praying for something for a long while and our prayers have not been answered. Maybe where we have believed for something that God has promised in His Word and yet our situation remains unchanged. It's then that disappointment, if we allow it, will start to eat away at us, frustrating and discouraging our lives. The affect of such disappointment is spoken of in the Bible when it says,
> "Hope deferred makes the heart sick, but a desire fulfilled is a tree of life." (Proverbs 13:12)

In spite of all this potential frustration, the good news is that lasting fulfilment is at the heart of the gospel! Jesus said,
> "I came that they may have and enjoy life, and have it in abundance-to the full, till it overflows."
> (John 10:10b, Amp)

This is why the message of Jesus is as relevant today as when it was first spoken. It meets the deepest need within the heart of every person; that need to be fulfilled!

Having considered some of the major causes of frustration, let us now look more closely at the gift of fulfilment that God wants each one of us to enjoy. In John 7:37-43 Jesus speaks to a world in search of satisfaction and to a people thirsting to find fulfilment:

> *"On the last day of the feast, the great day, Jesus stood up and proclaimed, "If any one thirst, let him come to me and drink. He who believes in me, as the scripture has said, 'Out of his heart shall flow rivers of living water.'" Now this He said about the Spirit, which those who believed in Him were to receive; for as yet the Spirit had not been given, because Jesus was not yet glorified. When they heard these words, some of the people said, "This is really the prophet." Others said, "This is the Christ." But some said, "Is the Christ to come from Galilee? Has not the scripture said that the Christ is descended from David, and comes from Bethlehem, the village where David was?" So there was a division among the people over Him."*

The people in this passage made different choices over what they heard and saw concerning Christ, and the same thing happens today. Invariably, whenever the message of Christ is presented, particularly when it relates to the Holy Spirit, there will arise a division among people over Him. This is not simply the case with regards to the unconverted; it is also true of those who call themselves *'believers'*, within the Church. The fact is, if you are determined to fulfil your own destiny, and want to help others find theirs, you will not be able to please everyone. Division over what you have discovered and want to share will arise and you will not always be accepted. Jesus Himself said,

> *"... I have not come to bring peace, but a sword."*
> (Matthew 10:34b)

Also in verse 36 the Lord made clear that,
> *"... a man's foes will be those of his own household."*

The perception that a person has, of any situation, considerably influences their choices and the reactions they make. From the passage in John chapter 7, we notice the response of three different kinds of people:

(a) Those That Saw Partially: The response of the first group was to say, *"This is really the Prophet."* While they were stirred and excited by what they could see in Jesus, and their conclusion was right, they had limited themselves because they were only partially right. Jesus, of course, was far more than just a prophet.

(b) Those That Saw Perfectly: These people announced with great conviction, *"This is the Christ!"* By revelation their eyes were opened and their hearts were moved because they saw Jesus not merely as a good man, or teacher, and certainly not just as a prophet. They could see Jesus as the Messiah, the anointed one sent by God - The Christ!

(c) Those That Saw Like The Pharisees: This group was full of knowledge, but had no revelation. So preoccupied were they with being 'correct' that their legalistic concern for detail was obscuring the discovery of the truth that was standing right before them. They had distanced themselves from the enthusiasm of the other two groups and were trying to sow doubt, pouring cold water on their excitement. Their response was,

"Is the Christ to come from Galilee? Has not the scripture said that the Christ is descended from David, and comes from Bethlehem, the village where David was?"

They were so busy trying to understand with logic and reason that they couldn't see or enter into what others were enjoying.

In any congregation, and indeed even in the readership of this book, these same three categories exist today. To progress in finding fulfilment and discover our destiny we must recognise in which group we are:

Those that understand *Partially;* - They have a blurred, limited perception, but at least they have a sincere openness of heart and a teachable spirit. Those that see *Perfectly;* - They are quick to embrace the revelation of God with enthusiasm and faith, boldly declaring what they know to be true. And those who react like the **Pharisee;** - They interpret spiritual truth with a legalistic attitude and as a result miss the substance of God's presence. The mechanics of a religious framework are there, but not the dynamics of a relational friendship with the person of the Holy Spirit. As a result they not only hold back themselves, criticising and being negative; they also consider it their religious duty to stop others getting too excited as well!

In considering this passage from John chapter 7, there are four steps necessary for us to choose to take if we want to move into a deeper revelation of Christ and an experience of lasting fulfilment. Without moving along this path and taking each one of these steps, frustration will continue in our lives.

Firstly, Decide To Acknowledge Our Need

Jesus said, *"If <u>any one thirst</u>....."* It is so easy to cover up and make excuses, or react defensively. However, the first thing that we must do if we are to find true fulfilment, is to acknowledge that it is ourselves that this part of God's Word applies to. By holding up our hand and admitting, *'It's me Jesus is speaking about,'* will be the beginning of knowing a new walk with the Lord. Just like the words of the old Negro spiritual song: "It's not my brother, or my sister, it's me standing in the need of prayer!" We will never really drink in a way that brings fulfilment until we first acknowledge we are thirsty. We must recognise where we are at the moment and decide it is not where we want to remain. The path to fulfilment begins when we understand that it is not primarily our circumstances or other people that need to change, it is ourselves!

Three years ago I had the opportunity to take a month's Sabbatical away from twenty-two years of full-time ministry. For part of that time I travelled to the Airport Christian Fellowship in Toronto, Canada, one of the revival centres of the world. The purpose for going was because I was thirsty and I wanted to seek God for a fresh revelation of His presence, that He might accomplish a new work in my heart and life. The name Toronto means 'Meeting Place' and that is just what it was for myself and has been for more than four million other people who have visited that church, in the period of seven years since the revival began in 1995. The reason why so many have travelled from all over the world, even from some of the most obscure nations on the globe, has been because of a spiritual thirst. At the time of writing the church still meets every night except Mondays, and people continue to travel thousands of miles because they are thirsty!

One of the most astonishing things, so evident in every meeting, was the readiness of people to respond and acknowledge that they were in need of prayer. Each evening, after the message was preached, an opportunity for people to do something about what they had heard was given and immediately over 95% of the congregation flooded forward to receive ministry! There was no need for a second invitation; no begging and pleading for people to come forward; instantly individuals stepped out because they were eager to meet with God.

The main obstacle, more than anything else, which keeps a person from finding fulfilment, is lack of motivation to change. This is where people make a decision to put off till another day the thing God is saying to them. What happens then is that the days run into the weeks, the weeks into the months and the months run into the years. The Word God has challenged them about and what He has put His finger on in their lives they decide to push to the back of their minds and do nothing. That one decision, time and time again, robs people of so much, not least the opportunity to discover their true destiny!

I'm told that in one particular coffee shop in America they have a very clever advertising gimmick to attract customers into their store. Outside and above the shop there is a large billboard that in big, bold, back letters announces, **'FREE COFFEE SERVED HERE TOMORROW!'** People see this and realising that you don't get much free in life they turn up the following day to the store. Then just as they are about to go in and claim their free drink, they look up and read the poster, only to see it still has the same message of promise: TOMORROW!

We can so easily deceive, not only other people, but also ourselves in a similar way, because in a sense tomorrow never comes, particularly when we put off until another day what we ought to be acting upon immediately. The Bible tells us, *"… Today, when you hear His voice, do not harden hearts…."* (Hebrews 3:15). The time to respond to the Lord is when He speaks and if we don't, what actually happens is a hardening of our hearts occurs. Almost without us noticing it we begin to lose our sensitivity to the Holy Spirit and even though we might be busy with religious activity, little by little our hearts become hardened to what God is saying.

It is interesting to notice the timing of when Jesus announced this invitation for the thirsty to come to Him. We see in verse 37 that it was at the height of a religious celebration:
>"*On the last day of the feast, the great day, Jesus stood up and proclaimed 'If any one thirst'......*"

The feast referred to here was the 'Feast of Tabernacles.' It was an extremely important feast to the Jews. These were very religious people that Jesus was addressing. They had travelled many miles to be there for this event, because it was one of the most important feasts in the Jewish calendar.

I don't believe they were all hypocrites by any means. They were sincere, God-fearing Jews, who loved the Feast of Tabernacles. One of the things, though, that we know only too well about the heart of Jesus, is that He always speaks to our deepest need. Amidst all the religious fervour and activity taking place on that occasion, and when these people had been as religious as they possibly could have been - *"On the **last** day of the feast..."* - Jesus chooses that moment to speak about spiritual issues.

Our deepest need is certainly not to be more religious: to read our Bibles longer, pray harder, attend more meetings, or increase our financial giving. Being religious can never bring fulfilment. This satisfaction can only be found when we are responding to God and we know the reality of intimacy with Him. The deepest need that we have, therefore, is for a close personal relationship with Jesus Christ, which is why He begins this gracious invitation with the words, *"If any one thirst...."*

We can be thirsty for many different reasons: (a) it could be because we have little or no relationship with Jesus. (b) We might be in a wilderness spiritually where we're going through a dry, hard and barren time: having taken a few knocks we're discouraged and feel as though we have lost our way. (c) Perhaps we are thirsty simply because we just want more of God and long to know a closer sense of His presence, a greater anointing of His Holy Spirit, a clearer understanding of His will for our lives, a deeper prayer life or more effective ministry. Whatever the cause of our thirst, the first important step along the pathway to fulfilment is that we make a decision to acknowledge our need.

Secondly, **Determine To Seek After Christ**

It is a great temptation for people to seek after the spectacular, or the latest exciting phenomena in Church-life today. With the many 'big names' and charismatic ministries to choose from, there is an attraction to be so taken up in pursuing *'power encounters'* and a *'quick fix'* for our needs to be met, that we don't seek after the person of Christ. So easily we can get sidetracked from finding a deeper relationship with Jesus by being distracted with the sensational. Also in our search for success, recognition, appreciation, love and security there is the temptation to look to other people or other things rather than to look first to Christ. These specific words of Jesus, therefore, are as important for Christians today, as when they were initially spoken: *"If any one thirst, let him* **come to me and drink***..."*

There is no substitute for this personal Christ-centeredness. In fact to thirst without first coming to Christ leads only to deception, disappointment and danger. Our response must always be to seek after Christ and not to set our expectation on anything else. One of the things that impressed me so much about my visit to Toronto was to see how centred on Jesus everything was. In fact I've never, in all the thousands of meetings that I've attended over the years, been anywhere that was more Christ-centred. In each service every night, throughout all the worship, testimonies and preaching, it was Jesus from beginning to end who was being presented, magnified and exalted. Imperfect as our efforts might be at times, we can't go far wrong, if as best as we know how, we are seeking to make Jesus pre-eminent in all things!

This characteristic became particularly evident to me when one night there was no 'well known' speaker on the platform. Instead someone spoke who by no stretch of the imagination was a preacher; in fact he was quite dull and uninteresting to listen to. In view of this I was curious to see what would happen when he came to the end of his message and gave the invitation for people to respond. That moment arrived and he proceeded to make a short, straightforward appeal. Listening to him, I thought to myself that there was little chance of anyone coming out for prayer. However, as soon as he gave the invitation hundreds immediately flooded forward in response! It quickly became obvious, in a way that I've never seen before, that people were not concerned about who was preaching, or how well he had spoken, nor was there any pressure of emotional manipulation to respond. Everyone present was there sincerely to meet only with Jesus, and came forward with the motivation to yield their lives to Him.

This right attitude of heart is crucial if we are to seek after Christ and know Him in a deeper more meaningful way. We therefore must be prepared to:

(a) **Repent Of Criticism:** There are those today who have a critical spirit and speak in an extremely negative way, expressing their views and opinions on anything new or different that they feel uncomfortable with. This is particularly so when they view the earnest spiritual thirst of others and feel embarrassed or awkward by the total abandonment to God that they observe in them. Such criticism is usually a smoke-screen for people's 'spiritual bankruptcy,' hiding their own lack of desire and liberty.

Without a right attitude of heart it is impossible to find true fulfilment because of the conflicts that are going on inside. The attitude of the Psalmist best expresses what God requires. David says,

"Thou has said, 'Seek ye my face.' My heart says to thee, 'Thy face, Lord, do I seek'." (Psalm 27:8)

When we are truly seeking the face of God we won't be concerned about what others are doing, or what may or may not be going on around us. If we are really steadfastly looking to the Lord and are occupied with Him, nothing else will be of concern to us.

(b) **Be Wholehearted:** Another attitude that is so important is unreserved resolve. Our lives must express the sort of commitment which indicates that whatever it costs and whatever it takes, we are going to seek the Lord. His promise is,

"... you will seek the Lord your God, and you will find Him, if you search after Him with all your heart and with all your soul." (Deuteronomy 4:29)

We will never be able to drift *into* a deeper relationship with anyone. We can certainly drift *out* of one, but it never occurs the other way round. We have to settle the issue within ourselves and decide to be 100% determined to move into where God wants us to be.

The examples found in God's Word reveal this passionate pursuit and are a great challenge to us:

"As the deer longs for flowing streams, so longs my soul for thee, O God." (Psalm 42:1)

"O God, thou art my God. I seek thee, my soul thirsts for thee; my flesh faints for thee, as in a dry and weary land where no water is." (Psalm 63:1)

"How lovely is thy dwelling place, O Lord of hosts! My soul longs, yea, faints for the courts of the Lord...." (Psalm 84:1 & 2)

(c) **Make Some Sacrifice:** If we are determined and really mean it, then that commitment will result in us moving out of our 'comfort zone' and making some sacrifice that is costly. There are two very important words that Jesus spoke in John chapter 7 which express this responsibility on our part:

*"If any one thirst, let him **come** to me and **drink**......"*

The words *'come'* and *'drink'* speak about a decision we need to make; it presents us with a choice to put ourselves out and do something; - or just wait and stay as we are.

A person doesn't need to get on a plane and fly thousands of miles to Toronto or any other place of revival to meet with God in a deeper way. For myself, though, it was an opportunity for me to express to God that no sacrifice was too great and no cost too high. With others it might not mean travelling thousands of miles; for them it could simply be the distance of their knees to the floor in earnest prayer. It need not mean going to another country, but simply moving into another room, away from distractions, to be alone and still before the Lord. The principle is clear though, if we are wholehearted we will decide to make some sacrifice and do something!

Should we ever get the opportunity however, to visit a place where revival is present, I would certainly recommend it; this doesn't take anything away from our commitment to our own local church. Nor should it diminish our expectation for what God can do right where we are. It is just an opportunity to put ourselves out and make some form of sacrifice to express the sincerity of our faith. When we look at past revivals we find that the earnest seeking heart will always be prepared to willingly make whatever sacrifice is necessary.

One good example of this was during the Welsh Revival of 1904 when there was a tremendous move of God across the land. At that time there was an Anglican minister by the name of Alexander Body who was vicar in charge of a church in Sunderland. He got to hear about the revival that was making such an impact on people and so his congregation sent him across to see for himself what was happening. He travelled over to Wales and his life was transformed as God mightily met with him there. He then returned to Sunderland and not long afterwards the great Sunderland revival broke out under his ministry.

During this period an uneducated plumber from Bradford heard of how the Spirit was being poured out in Sunderland. This man decided that he would go and find out what was taking place. He travelled from Bradford to Sunderland and it was there that he was baptised in the Holy Spirit and the outstanding world–wide ministry of Smith Wigglesworth began with miraculous signs and wonders!

In both of these cases, for Alexander Body and Smith Wigglesworth, God could have touched and changed their lives in their own churches, or at least in their own towns. However, God chose to honour those who with all their hearts were making some sacrifice in seeking after Him, and He will do the same for us today if we will but make that bold decision to show the same earnest intent.

Thirdly, Depend Entirely On God's Word

In this day and age where there is a great deal of deception to watch out for, it is vital that we have our faith grounded on what

the scriptures say and not merely on personal experiences or other people's testimonies. The words of Jesus in John chapter 7 must form the basis of our expectation; otherwise we will be left frustrated and lacking fulfilment. Jesus said,
> "If any one thirst, let him come to me and drink. He who believes in me, **as the scripture has said**....."

It is not a case of believing anything and everything that people tell us, or embracing whatever is done in the name of Christianity; we must depend completely upon what God's Word says and let the scriptures be our final authority.

Here again is another major reason why people lack fulfilment today, because they are building their expectations on what God has not said. Jesus tells us,
> "Many false prophets will arise and lead many astray."   (Matthew 24:11)

And again in verse 24 He says,
> "For false Christs and false prophets will arise and show great signs and wonders, so as to lead astray, if possible, even the elect."

There is always the very real danger of being drawn into things that are either a counterfeit distraction of the enemy, or simply the clamour of the flesh life for the sensational. For this reason caution is certainly needed.

The gift of prophecy is one of the important and powerful ways God moves us forward to fulfil our destiny; it is also, though, an area of great danger because people, no matter how well meaning, can get it wrong and do make mistakes. Therefore, if we are building our hopes on something that is encouraging, which we want to hear, but it hasn't come from God, then we are not only going to be disappointed and frustrated, we are likely also to miss our true destiny. The Word of God must always be our final authority, which is why Jesus said,
> "Man shall not live by bread alone, but by every word that proceeds from the mouth of God."   (Matthew 4:4)

I personally know of a church in Devon where the Pastor one day declared to his congregation that he had received a *"Word from the Lord!"* According to this 'revelation' they were to sell their building and embark on a massive project to build a multipurpose venue that would be used by the community and make a significant impact on the area. A glossy brochure was printed, an expensive professional video promoting the vision was produced, and surveyor's plans were drawn up. The church had spent several thousand pounds on the vision and had committed themselves to spend a considerable amount more.

This project was not only something that excited the church; it was also featured in the local newspapers and was becoming the talk of the town. Then, without any warning, the Pastor gave notice to the church that he was leaving them and taking up a new appointment overseas! This was a huge shock to those left. As a result the vision was aborted, the congregation was disappointed and frustrated and the good name of the church among the other churches and also in the community was tarnished. Such a lot of damage was caused because of someone who had a good idea, but convinced himself and everyone else that it was *"The Word of the Lord!"*

There are sufficient principles in God's Word to keep us safe from deception and give us a solid and sure foundation to our lives. When we are obeying what is clearly revealed already, and our lives are submitted to the authority of the scriptures, then when the time comes for us to launch out in faith, pressing forward to realise our destiny, we will do so with greater confidence and security. Also, in developing our expectation, God is clear in His word about things like healing, liberty in praise and worship, spiritual gifts, supernatural power and ability. He wants us to believe Him for greater things than we have received and to build our lives on those promises. In doing so, we will enter a whole new dimension of living.

If we truly did *"believe as the scriptures have said"* it wouldn't be an overstatement to say that our lives would be dramatically transformed and we would never be the same again! Apply this principle to what the scriptures have to say for example about Jesus Christ, ourselves, and the devil and it becomes a tremendous challenge to us:

(a) **Jesus Christ:** The scriptures present Jesus not only as Saviour from sin, but also as our Provider, Comforter, Councillor, Everlasting Father, Prince of Peace, The

Mighty God, Healer of sickness, Deliverer from oppression and the one who guides us through life etc. In fact the scriptures say, *"Jesus Christ is the same yesterday and today and forever."* (Hebrews 13:8). If we truly believed this we would have a greater expectation for the miraculous in our services and no anxiety about anything in our daily lives. We would also have a tremendous confidence and excitement about passing on such a discovery to everyone we met.

(b) **Ourselves:** Too often and for too long we have allowed the enemy to rob us of how we should be living. In the light of God's Word though, when we believe what the scriptures say we find our true identity and calling. Jesus said,
> *"He who believes in me will also do the works that I do; and greater works than these will he do…."*
> (John 14:12)

The apostle John taught,
> *"… greater is He that is in you, than he that is in the world."* (1 John 4:4, AV)

Paul says that God has,
> *"… blessed us in Christ with every spiritual blessing in the heavenly places."* (Ephesians 1:3)

King David reveals the Lord's favour and blessing on man:
> *"Thou hast made him little less than God, and dost crown him with glory and honour. Thou hast given him dominion over the works of thy hands; thou hast put all things under his feet…."*
> (Psalm 8:5 & 6)

It is by believing as the scriptures have said, that our lives dramatically begin to change!

(c) **The Devil:** There are two extremes in the church today, both of which are contrary to the teaching of God's Word. On the one hand we have those who are completely oblivious to any demonic activity. They have no idea as to who it is behind the attack upon their health, marriage, family, finances, ministry etc. Although the apostle Paul said in 2 Corinthians 2:11, *"... for we are not ignorant of his devices,"* there is an appalling lack of understanding among many Christians as to the very real spiritual conflict that we are in. This is so even when God's Word tells us,

> *"We are not contending against flesh and blood, but against the principalities, against the powers, against the world rulers of this present darkness, against the spiritual hosts of wickedness in the heavenly places."* (Ephesians 6:12)

If we truly believed this, we'd certainly pray and live a lot differently to how we often do.

The other extreme is where we have Christians who see a demon in everything that moves! The devil gets blamed for anything that is going wrong in their lives. If we believed though, as the scriptures have said, we would live in a way that demonstrates the devil is a defeated foe and that he is underneath our feet! Rather than being preoccupied, looking over our shoulder in case of attack, confessing, *"Oh, the devil's at me today!"* we would have the devil on the run!

Fourthly, Desire To Meet The Needs Of Others

We might well have everything clearly in place that has been mentioned so far, but unless this final point is something we have made a conscious decision to believe for, then we will never realise our true destiny, and as a consequence it will be impossible to be fulfilled. The importance of this is seen in the words of Jesus, when He said in John chapter 7,

> *"If any one thirst, let him come to me and drink......**Out of his heart shall flow rivers of living water**."*

Here we have another major reason for lack of fulfilment in the lives of Christians - self-centredness. Whenever we are turned in on ourselves, pre-occupied with our own problems and needs, we will be frustrated!

The reason for such frustration is because we have been created and called to be servants of Christ, reflecting His glorious self-less nature that consistently reaches out to meet the needs of other people. Those who ought to be most affected by us are our husband/wife, our children, those within the church, colleagues that we work with, and our next-door neighbours. Jesus said, *"... freely ye have received, freely give."* (Matthew 10:8, AV). Any personal revival within ourselves should auto-matically result in a passion to reach others, in the same way that the genuineness of Isaiah's encounter with the Lord compelled him to answer the call of God and respond, *"Here I am! Send me."* (Isaiah 6:8b).

Where a river has no outlet, then the waters will soon become stagnant. This is something that can happen in the church today. There may be many activities taking place and numerous meetings going on, but if evangelism isn't one of the top priorities then eventually the church will become like a stagnant pool where little new life is evident. This also is part of the reason why many revivals 'fizzle out'. No matter how great and powerful the moving of God's Holy Spirit might be upon a congregation, if it doesn't turn people outward to share what they have received and know of the gospel, then it will not only be short lived and lost, it might even be counterproductive!

In John chapter 4, with the woman of Samaria, we notice that she was thirsty not only for natural water, but there was an inner thirst for fulfilment going on within her personal life. Jesus therefore spoke to her about *'spiritual water'* and her need to drink from a Spiritual well that would never run dry. He made the statement,

"... whoever drinks of the water that I shall give him will never thirst again...."   (verse 14)

She was searching for satisfaction but was looking in the wrong place. We see this in that she'd had five husbands and the man she was living with was not her husband. The wrong choices she had been making were not only bringing frustration and dissatisfaction to herself, they were causing her to miss her God-given destiny! However, her encounter with Jesus was so powerful, that she dropped the water jar, ran back to her village and shared with others the good news of her changed life. What she had received flowed out from her with such enthusiasm that, many others believed and found Christ as their Saviour.

This is exactly what Jesus wants to do in our own lives; send us out to be a blessing to everyone we meet as we simply let the discovery we've made flow naturally out from us. If *"Rivers of living water"* are issuing out of your innermost being you can be sure of this: you will know it, and others will notice it! How can it be anything other than this? We are bound to feel the difference and others will always receive the benefit. Notice God's Word in John chapter 7 speaks not about a "trickle," or even one river flowing out from us; it refers to *"Rivers!"* Such an experience will be impossible to hide!

When the Bible talks about rivers flowing out of those who have received from God, at least two things should immediately become evident; there will be new attitudes and new activity:

(a) **New Attitudes:** In Galatians 5:22 & 23 Paul makes clear what these attitudes are. As the Holy Spirit fills the life of the believer, then flowing out from them will come the characteristics of Christ: *"Love, joy, peace, patience, kindness, goodness, faithfulness, gentleness, and self-control."* Others will notice because they'll be seeing a change that stands out. With a puzzled look they will start to think there's something different about that person; they aren't so irritable as they used to be. They have more patience and are more thoughtful and loving than they've ever been before. Their conclusion will be that something has happened, even though they may not know quite what it is!

(b) **New Activity:** The Holy Ghost will always bring a Holy Go! A new dynamic of passion will be evident, bringing motivation in service. Not merely making us busy doing 'good things', but causing us to be occupied with God-given objectives - activities that will make a difference for eternity. This was seen in the life and ministry of Jesus whose priority was to, *"seek and save the lost."* (Luke 19:10)

General William Booth, founder of the Salvation Army, had the same consuming priority. He was someone from whom the rivers of God's Holy Spirit never cease to flow toward others. One day he had an audience with King Edward VII, who highly commended his unflagging zeal and work among the poor. Booth's reply to the king's glowing words was straightforward and sincere: "Your Majesty, some men's passion is for art. Some men's passion is for fame. My passion is for souls!"

There are many reasons that Christians give for their reluctance to be involved in evangelism. Any person though that does not have a desire to evangelise will always lack fulfilment. This is simply because they are not engaged in their God-given destiny to be a witness for Christ. We have been called and commissioned by Jesus to spread the gospel and make disciples. We haven't got to wait for a word saying, *"Go"* - that has been given to us already! We should be going until we have a word from God to say, *"Stop!"* or *"Stay!"*

In conclusion: the promise of fulfilment is the Lord's provision for every Christian and an essential part of being able to discover and pursue our destiny. Where we have areas of frustration in our lives we must see the importance of making the right choices. Therefore let us:

Firstly - **Decide To Acknowledge Our Need:** When we hear Jesus asking, *"If anyone is thirsty?"* our decision needs to be, to respond in openness and honesty, indicating that we can identify with being the one who His invitation applies to.

Secondly - **Determine To Seek After Christ:** In listening to Jesus say, *"Let him come to me and drink,"* we must choose to look nowhere else for fulfilment, but to rise up from where we are, make some effort and wholeheartedly pursue a deeper relationship with the Lord, regardless of the cost.

Thirdly - **Depend Entirely On God's Word:** Where deception is all around, we need to daily make the choice to be alert and cautious about error. At the same time though, also decide to accept the challenge to, *"believe as the scriptures have* *said"* - starting with those things the Bible tells us about <u>Jesus,</u> <u>ourselves</u> and the <u>devil</u>.

Fourthly **-** **Desire To Meet The Needs Of Others:** Avoiding the temptation to be self-centred, we choose to reach out beyond ourselves, so that we are not only blessed, but we want to be a blessing everywhere we go. Our prayer should be that, *"out of our heart will flow rivers of living water."*

Chapter 5

Choosing To Live By The Transforming Power Of Faith

We live in a culture today where people want to change and improve their lives in a variety of ways. The rich spend thousands of pounds on cosmetic surgery to achieve that *'perfect look.'* For some, great effort is made to keep fit, or diet and lose weight seeking that *'perfect shape.'* While others attend hundreds of hours in counselling, to overcome deep-rooted and debilitating problems, in search of that *'perfect answer.'*

In our 'image conscious,' 'achievement driven,' society there is enormous pressure on people to succeed, to be accepted and to *'fit in.'* Invariably though, the mistake that is made, is looking for change to come on a superficial level, from some 'quick-fix' plan, or in guidance based on humanistic philosophy. True and lasting change, however, must start from within, and always begins with our relationship to God.

Most of us have things about ourselves that we'd like to alter; circumstances we need to rise above, or barriers we want to break through and overcome. This can be the case in areas like lack of confidence and insecurity, ill health, financial difficulties, sinful habits, conflict in relationships, discouragement in ministry, exasperation in business etc. Without overstating the point, God has given us the most powerful spiritual force in the universe so that we might experience change and always live in victory; it is the power of Faith! His Word says,

"... *this is the victory that overcomes the world, our faith."* (1 John 5:4b)

Let us consider then how life-changing this can be as we examine three things about faith:

Firstly, Faith Is A Positive Power

Everything about faith gives reassurance; it miraculously transforms every negative into a positive, and there are plenty of negatives in life today. We could no doubt make a long list of the stressful things that affect our lives right now. Regardless of how distressing they may be though, we are not left helpless and at their mercy.

Just recently I was ministering at a meeting in the south where I met an extraordinary example of this. Among those who came forward for prayer was a young mother and her two small boys who, a few months earlier, had all been hospitalised having narrowly escaped being murdered by the woman's husband. He had repeatedly stabbed them in a frenzied attack, then fled from the scene and committed suicide by throwing himself off the nearby cliffs. Despite this appallingly negative situation, it was remarkable to see the mother's faith unshaken. There was no sign of any bitterness towards her husband for what he had done, nor any sense of accusation against God, asking why this had happened to them. Instead there was an attitude of faith as she sought prayer that the Lord would heal the emotional trauma of such an experience.

Whatever circumstances life might throw at us, they will probably rarely be as negative as the one I've just mentioned. No matter how difficult they may be, we can live with the assurance that faith powerfully changes Defeat into Victory, - Fear into Confidence, - Bondage into Liberty, - Sickness into Health, - Failure into Success, - Poverty into Prosperity, - Discouragement into Zeal, - Despair into Hope, - Frustration into Fulfilment, - Sadness into Joy, and so much more! In fact there is no negative that faith cannot transform and bring some good out of in time.

This power only becomes a reality, though, when we take a determined stand and refuse to allow any negative influence to affect our lives. The old popular song, written by Johny Mercer and made famous by Bing Crosby puts it so well, we need to, *"Accentuate the positive, eliminate the negative, latch on to the affirmative, and don't mess with Mr In-between."* Each one of us must choose to settle in our hearts that our faith will not be dominated by feeling, dictated to by facts, or deluded by fantasy.

(a) **Dominated By Feelings:** Our emotions can have an extremely negative effect upon us if we allow them to. They cannot be trusted because they are fickle and fluctuate so much. Frequently other people, our personal circumstances, the moodiness of our own personality, and even the weather influence our faith! When we are dominated by feelings it is like being on an emotional roller coaster which throws us up and down from ecstasy to depression, confidence to fearfulness, assurance to doubt etc.

(b) **Dictated To By Facts:** Although certain facts might be very real and undeniable, they are not the final authority in our lives. Faith is able to change even the most indisputable facts! This is so whether those facts come in the form of a financial statement from the bank about lack of funds; the verdict of a doctor offering little hope for our sickness; the disinterest of an unsaved partner, or rebellious children that are backslidden etc. When the facts of our problems loom before us, shouting out a negative message of doubt, faith enables us to refuse to listen, because our ear is tuned to another pitch. Faith does not necessarily ignore the facts, but it ignores the power of the facts on our lives.

(c) **Deluded By Fantasy:** God has given us the wonderful gift of imagination, and when it is surrendered to Him it can be extremely positive and creative. However, if this is left unrestrained it can lead to a form of escapism and self-deception as well as being potentially destructive. We must never allow our faith to be deluded by grandiose thoughts, wishful thinking, or impetuous ideas, for these will always prove to be unfruitful and keep us from living in reality.

Deceiving spirits will often try to exploit this area of fantasy. Frequently I come across the casualties of this problem; those who embark on a particular course of action, declaring confidently one moment that the Lord has told them to do something, only to find them deciding when things get difficult that the Lord has told them to do something else! The negative results of such delusion for the individual concerned will always be frustration and disappointment, and the repercussion for others affected can be even more damaging.

Secondly, Faith Is A Personal Power

Although we can be encouraged, strengthened and helped by the example of other people's faith, we can't *'live off'* someone else's faith. I've heard some people remark that they wish they had the same faith as Benny Hinn, Reinhard Bonnke, or Billy Graham. The truth is though, we do have that same faith; in fact, dare I say we have the same faith as Jesus Christ Himself. The difference is how we personally apply that faith to the challenges and opportunities that life presents us with. The Bible tells us in Romans 12:3b,

> "... *God has dealt to every man the measure of faith.*" (AV)

We all have the ability to believe. Every time we get aboard a plane to go on holiday we exercise great faith by putting our life in the hands of the pilot. If ever we have to go into hospital for an operation we put our faith in the expertise of the surgeon. It's the same in everyday life; we need to apply that God-given power personally.

Consider how you initially came into a relationship with Christ: firstly, you recognised your need; secondly, you heard the most amazing promises made to you from the Bible; and thirdly, you personally applied those promises by faith to your life. The result was your life was remarkably changed; you came into relationship with the Lord who fills the entire universe and you were wonderfully born again! That is how we must continue to live each day of our lives as Christians:

> "*As therefore you received Christ Jesus the Lord, so live in Him....*"   (Colossians 2:6)

This is particularly important when we are reminded that the Bible says,

> "*Without faith it is impossible to please God.*"
> (Hebrews 11:6, NIV)

The way we make faith an active, personal power is by bringing into line with God's Word the areas of:

(a) **How We Think:** Paul reminds us in 2 Corinthians 10:5b about the personal responsibility we have in the 'battleground' of our minds to *"... take every thought captive to obey Christ."* Also in Romans 12:2b, he says, *"...be transformed by the renewal of your mind...."* No one else can do this for us; we must choose to take action ourselves. This is not the power of positive thinking, of mind over matter; it is simply bringing our lives into line with what God's Word says so that we begin to think: "I am who God says I am!" – "I have what God says I have!" and - "I can do what God says I can do!" It is the difference between waking up in the morning, looking out of the window, and thinking -"Good morning *Lord!"* or getting up thinking - "Good Lord, *morning!"*

(b) **How We Feel:** In Psalm 42:5, we see that the psalmist David brought his emotions into line with what it meant to live in victory when he said,
"Why are you cast down, O my soul, and why are you disquieted within me? Hope in God; for I shall again praise Him...."

This isn't simply saying, "Pull yourself together" or, "Snap out of it!" Rather it is reminding ourselves that our only help is found by turning to God. On another occasion, David and his army returned from battle to a place called Ziklag, only to find that the Amalekites had made a raid on their home. The enemy had burned it down and carried off their wives, sons and daughters. Not only had he to cope with the distress of the personal loss of his loved ones, but also on top of this, his own men were blaming him and spoke of stoning him. However, David's reaction is seen in 1 Samuel 30:6b:
"....David encouraged and strengthened himself in the Lord his God." (Amp)

(c) **How We Speak:** The effect of our own words, and the confession we make, will not only have an impact on other people, but can bring spiritual life or death upon ourselves. If we constantly respond to difficult situations by saying how hopeless a problem is, or that there's no way out of what is confronting us, we can bring to pass what we say in our own lives and damage our confidence. In the simplest of ways it is possible to undermine our faith. For example, if we make a mistake and are in the habit of reacting to the situation by saying, "What a fool I am!" or "How stupid of me to have done that!" - without realising it we are demolishing our own security.

Jesus taught how we can change our circumstances by speaking out in faith when He said in Mark 11:23,

"Truly, I say to you, whoever says to this mountain, 'Be taken up and cast into the sea', and does not doubt in his heart, but believes that what he says will come to pass, it will be done for him."

Therefore, if we are to live in victory we must make the decision to change our negative confession to a positive confession of faith. This is something we need to choose to do, not just on Sundays, or when we are around other Christians, but throughout our daily lives.

(d) **How We Act:** In John 2:5, Mary's instructions to the servants, when the wine had run out at a wedding in Cana were very simple: *"Do whatever He tells you."* The word *"Whatever"* is extremely important because at times the Lord will tell us to do some very strange things and we must take care that we don't hold back, hesitating, and in so doing, miss our miracle. The directions of Jesus for them to fill 6 large stone jars, and then present them at the wedding as the best wine, must have sounded very bizarre. Invariably, though, we find throughout the Bible that the Miraculous is often preceded by the Ridiculous.

There are many such examples in scripture of those who decided to act on God's instructions, even when these seemed somewhat peculiar. For instance: in Joshua 6:3-5, Joshua was told to march with his army around the walls of Jericho once for six days and on the seventh day to march around them seven times. Then they were to expect the walls to fall when the priests blew on their trumpets and ram's horns and everyone raised a loud shout. Certainly not a conventional battle plan!

Also Gideon's strategy, given by God, to defeat an army of many thousands with a small band of three hundred was just as ridiculous. They had to surround the enemy's camp at night, put flaming torches in earthen pitchers, and then at a given signal they were to break the pitchers and shout,
"For the Lord and for Gideon!" (Judges 7:18)

The fishermen, after returning exhausted from fishing all night, were told to,
"... Put out into the deep and let down your nets for a catch." (Luke 5:4b)

And the disciples were instructed to feed four thousand hungry people with a few loaves and fishes (Mark 8:1-9). Such examples do bring a great challenge for us to act upon God's Word, without reservation, but the results will be amazing!

When we look at Paul's lifestyle, we see that the power of faith affected not only what he taught; it also transformed how he personally lived. This is why he thought, felt, spoke and acted in such a positive way, even in extremely difficult situations. His conviction was, *"I am more than a conqueror!"* – *"Christ always causes me to triumph!"* – *"I can do all things through Christ that strengthens me!"*

Thirdly, Faith Is A Perceptive Power

Faith looks further than the immediate, the tangible and the superficial. It sees beyond that which we receive through our natural senses and for this reason we need to examine more closely what we understand faith to be. God's definition of faith is always the best and certainly the most accurate. In Hebrews 11:1 He tells us,
"Now faith is the <u>assurance</u> of things <u>hoped for</u>, the <u>conviction</u> of things <u>not seen</u>."

We can establish from this statement that faith is a strong inner certainty of God's promised provision and purpose coming to pass, even though there may be no visible evidence. Faith is related to things unseen by the natural eye, therefore our victory is nothing to do with the circumstances around us, or the outward appearance of what we are facing.

This is particularly challenging when we think of how we pray for the need of revival in our nation, the need of our loved ones being converted or restored from backsliding, and also our own personal needs. Are we just praying prayers, or do we really pray in faith? Even when there is no visible difference, no concrete evidence and no obvious change, we must make a choice to believe God. In doing so we maintain, as we pray, a full assurance of what we hope for and a deep conviction of what we don't yet see. That is Bible faith; living with a conviction that it is going to happen.

The amazing thing is that living by faith actually gives us a 'second-sight.' We are able to view problems through the eyes of the Holy Spirit within us and see what others cannot see. This was the longing Paul had for the Ephesian Christians and why he spoke in prayer about them *"... having the eyes of their hearts enlightened...."* (Ephesians 1:18a). There are numerous examples in the Bible of people who, rather than living just by the information of what their natural eyes told them, lived according to the perceptive sight of faith:

(a) **Elisha** in 2 Kings 6:14 & 15 was facing enemy forces that were far greater in number than his own army and yet he confidently says, *"Fear not, for those who are with us are more than those who are with them."* (verse 16). This account goes on to reveal why Elisha was so secure in such an intimidating situation. He could see, 'in the Spirit,' that the great host of the armies of heaven were surrounding the enemy, (verse 17).

(b) **Paul** had good cause, on many occasions, to feel discouraged and give in to defeat because he faced so much opposition and many set-backs. However, he remained steadfast, refusing to lose heart, and we find the secret of his victory in the statement of faith he made in 2 Corinthians 4:18. He said, *"... we look not to the things that are seen, but to the things that are unseen...."*

(c) The Apostle John was exiled on the Island of Patmos when he was in his mid-eighties. Even though he was an elderly man, banished from his friends and family, we know that his faith was still evident, enabling him to overcome. He lived in a spiritual dimension that affected all he could see, which is why John could say in Revelation 1:10, *"I was in the Spirit on the Lord's day...."*

The dimension of faith is the realm that God always operates in, especially when raising up ordinary people to complete the most extraordinary tasks. He sees in us not merely what we are at the moment, but beyond that to all we shall become. It is for this reason we read in Romans 4:17 about,
> *"... the God who gives life to the dead and calls things that are not as though it were."* (NIV)

Such perception and faith is clearly illustrated in how God saw ordinary people becoming extraordinary and doing great exploits:

Gideon was trembling for fear, threshing out corn in a wine press, afraid of the Midianite army, and yet God's words to him were, *"... you mighty man of valour"* (Judges 6:12b). When God looked at Moses He didn't just see a man full of insecurities and deep inadequacies; He saw one of the world's most courageous ever leaders. With Jeremiah, He saw not just a child, but also a prophet that would shake nations. Peter, in the eyes of God, was seen not as a coward, but as someone who would preach to thousands and be one of the strong leaders of the New Testament Church. And with Saul of Tarsus, God could see not just a murderer, blasphemer and persecutor of the Christian Faith, but one of the greatest missionaries the Church has ever known.

It is encouraging to remind ourselves that the Lord also looks at us in the same way He looked at them. We are flawed and far from perfect, yet God looks at us with faith. His perception of our lives is viewed from the perspective of faith:
> *"The assurance of things hoped for and the conviction of things not yet seen."*

This is also the same way He expects us to live, in regards to how we view ourselves, our problems and other people. Though for this extraordinary power to actually change us, we must choose to maintain a faith that is:

(1) Focussed: We need to take steps and be responsible to make sure our faith isn't distorted or blurred in any way. If our faith isn't focussed, everything we look at will be vague and uncertain. Faith is kept focussed as we decide to look to **The Word of God** – reminding ourselves that it is eternal and unchanging; it still means the same today as it did when it was first spoken! It is also *"living and active."* Just as it was in the beginning of creation, still today there is a creative, life giving quality inherent in it. His unchanging, life-giving word is our stability and the source of our total supply. As we abide in Him and His Word abides in us it puts us in the position of being able to ask anything and we can expect to receive it!

Our faith is kept in sharp focus by reflecting on **The Character of God** – He is faithful and true; it is impossible for Him to lie and not honour His Word. He is steadfast in His love towards us and full of compassion. As our Heavenly Father He cares deeply about our frustrations and failures and is committed to our success. He is willing to answer our prayers and delights to bless us. In fact He is more willing to give than we are to receive, and always rewards those who diligently seek Him.

Also to have a faith that is focused clearly we need to dwell on **The Ability of God** – He is unlimited in His power and unequalled in His authority. He is a miracle-working God; nothing is ever too difficult for Him and His power is the same today as it has always been. When our faith is looking to His ability rather than our inability then we can expect the unexpected to happen!

(2) Fixed: Peter's extraordinary faith in walking on water is a good example of victory over incredible circumstances. While his faith was not only focussed but also fixed on Jesus, he was able to do the impossible. The moment he got distracted and looked around, doubt came in, and he began to be afraid and sink. This is why the Bible in Hebrews 12:2a directs us to live our lives, *"… looking to*

Jesus, the pioneer and perfecter of our faith." Our faith needs to be so fixed on Christ's word, character and ability that it is <u>firm</u>, <u>immovable</u>, and <u>unshakable</u>.

Abraham had a faith that was fixed concerning the miracle God had promised him of fathering children in his old age:

"He did not weaken in faith when he considered his own body, which was as good as dead because he was about a hundred years old, or when he considered the barrenness of Sarah's womb. No distrust made him waver concerning the promise of God, but he grew strong in his faith as he gave glory to God, fully convinced that God was able to do what He had promised."   (Romans 4:19-21)

The importance of fixing our faith in a determined way is taught in James 1:8. There it makes clear that if we have two minds about what we believe, then, not only will we be unstable in everything we do, but also we will not receive anything from the Lord. Single-minded certainty is central to faith. For us to be so resolute it is essential that we make a decision to disregard all other voices such as: <u>un-spiritual council</u>, - <u>internal doubts</u>, - <u>rational thinking</u>, - and the <u>whispers of Satan</u> for they will always weaken our determination and rob us of what God has said.

(3) **Fearless:** When our faith is focused and fixed it will, as a natural consequence, be fearless. There will be boldness, an audacity about our faith that leaves no room for doubt to develop into fear. Every time our faith is focussed and fixed we close the door to the opportunity of fear entering our lives. Fear can never have any access except through an open door. This amazing boldness is seen in the lives of people like David standing against Goliath, Daniel when faced with the den of lions and Shadrach, Meshach and Abednego as they were thrown into a fiery furnace. These men fearlessly thought, felt, spoke and acted according to what they believed, and as a result overcame the most terrifying of situations.

Who Can Experience This Transforming Power Of Faith?

Certainly not just a select few, like those in 'full-time ministry,' or the 'big names' in Christian service that we expect God to work powerfully through. Each one of us can be changed and released into a new realm of faith. The people who experience this are:

(a) **Those Who Have A Personal Relationship With God:** There are no exceptions; nobody need be excluded. The basic qualification necessary to experience victory is a living relationship with Christ as Lord. This is why we are told in 1 John 5:4a,
"Everyone born of God overcomes the world...."
(NIV)

Being born of God automatically gives us the right to use the name of Jesus and there is great power and promised blessing in His name. When Jesus spoke to His disciples about this He said that those who believed in the power of His name would see amazing 'signs and wonders:'
"... in my name they will cast out demons; they will speak in new tongues; they will pick up serpents, and if they drink any deadly thing, it will not hurt them; they will lay their hands on the sick, and they will recover." (Mark 16:17 & 18)

Once we come into a relationship with God, because we are His children, we are blessed with every spiritual blessing in Christ Jesus. As followers of Christ His name belongs to us and so do the riches of His provision through that name. Therefore we don't have to beg and plead for what we have already been provided with. Jesus said in John 15:16b,
"... the Father will give you whatever you ask in my name." (NIV)

For example, when we go to the bank to make a withdrawal, we don't say to the cashier, "Now I pray thee that thou wilt give me faith and ability and strength to write a cheque." We simply write the cheque and receive the money that is ours by drawing on the resources in our personal account. This is how we ought to be living in every-day life as we appropriate all that is ours in Christ!

(b) **Those Who Recognise What God Has Placed Within Them:** Too often we are preoccupied by thinking about what our painful past, difficult circumstances, other people and even what the devil has put within us. Instead we need to stop and recognise that which God has placed inside of us. The apostle Paul achieved the things he did because he understood the value and power of what God had deposited within the weakness of his life. He said in 2 Corinthians 4:7,
"We have this treasure in earthen vessels...."

His life reflected what he believed and so against all the devil could throw at him, to try and bring him defeat, he could say with confidence in verses 8 & 9,
"We are afflicted in every way, but not crushed; perplexed, but not driven to despair; persecuted, but not forsaken; struck down, but not destroyed."

The apostle John also lived by this same revelation which is why he said in 1 John 4:4, *"... for He who is in you is greater than he who is in the world."*

(c) **Those Who Feed Their Spirits On Godly Things:** How can we expect to overcome and live in victory if we are feeding off the 'garbage' of un-spiritual things that are offensive and contrary to God's nature. To be strong and live in victory we need a Godly diet, and be constantly feeding our spirits on things that are consistent with the character of God.

Faith *like* a mustard seed is all that is required to move mountains. This speaks not simply about the quantity, but the quality and the nature of faith. With the mustard seed there is a process, a development, and a progression. The same is true with faith. The more we feed, exercise and use it, the stronger and larger it grows. As we feed our faith our doubts will starve to death! Faith grows by feeding on: the <u>Presence of God</u> in our lives, the <u>Promises of God</u> to our lives, and the <u>Purpose of God</u> for our lives.

(d) Those Whose Response Demonstrates That No Situation Is Beyond Hope: Our response to the pressure that problems bring, soon reveals the kind of faith we have. It is in circumstances that appear unchangeable that we have the opportunity to let the power of faith overcome. A good example of this is Martha, when her brother Lazarus had been dead for four days. As soon as Jesus visited her she said to Him,

"Lord, if you had been here, my brother would not of died. But I know that even now God will give you whatever you ask." (John 11:21 & 22, NIV)

Martha's response to what seemed an impossible situation demonstrated that she believed, even though her brother was well beyond any human help, Jesus could bring him back to life again.

While this miracle happened over 2,000 years ago, God has not changed; He remains the same today and the power of faith is still able to accomplish the same remarkable transformation. A recent, well documented, modern-day resurrection, illustrates that fact:

On November 30th 2001, Nigerian pastor Daniel Ekechukwa, was delivering a Christmas present to his father, when the brakes of his car failed and he crashed into a stone pillar. Daniel suffered severe head injuries and heavy internal haemorrhaging. He was certified dead on arrival at the hospital, but his wife, Nneka, was convinced her husband would recover. This firm confidence came from the fact that God had impressed upon her the verse that said, *"Women received back their dead, raised to life again…."* (Hebrews 11:35a, NIV). She stubbornly held on to this and refused to let him be buried, (which usually would be done quickly in hot countries) so Daniel's body was injected with embalming fluid and left in the mortuary.

Eventually Nneka managed to persuade the mortician to release the body because she was intent on taking her dead husband to a healing meeting at which evangelist Reinhard Bonnke was preaching. They left the mortuary with the coffin and arrived at the service, only to be met by security officials who wouldn't allow it to be taken in, due to their suspicions that this might be a terrorist ploy. The determined wife however, persuaded them to let her take the coffin to a basement area of the church, where Christian staff kept guard over it.

These people could see clearly that rigor mortis had stiffened the limbs of the man, which were now like iron rods, but after a while the staff became aware that a slight twitching of the dead mans stomach was taking place. Then the corpse drew breath, followed shortly afterwards by irregular breathing. Finally, at 5.15 p.m. on Sunday December 2nd, Daniel opened his eyes and sat up. He asked for water and was carried to the main church sanctuary where hundreds of excited people saw him recover!

Today he is fit and healthy and travels widely, speaking of his amazing miracle. This transforming power of faith was experienced because of the persistence and determination of one woman who held on to God's Word, believing that no situation is beyond hope!

In conclusion: throughout the Bible, its message consistently declares, *"Faith is the victory that overcomes the world."* Where there are circumstances we need to rise above, barriers we need to break through and overcome, or areas of our lives that need to change, God can make a way where there seems to be no way. We just need to believe that with God <u>all</u> things are possible, and that they are possible for us, when we decide to live by faith as:

Firstly   -   A Positive Power.

Secondly   -   A Personal Power.

Thirdly   -   A Perceptive Power.

Chapter 6

Choosing To Be Free From The Ruin Of Regrets

In his autobiography, *'Just As I Am,'* Billy Graham tells about a conversation he had with President John F. Kennedy, shortly after his election, and the regret he felt resulting from that last meeting:

> "On the way back to the Kennedy house, the President-elect stopped the car and turned to me. "Do you believe in the Second Coming of Jesus Christ?" he asked unexpectedly.
>
> "I most certainly do," was my reply.
>
> "Well does *my* church believe it?"
>
> "They have it in their creeds."
>
> "They don't preach it," he said. "They don't tell us much about it. I'd like to know what you think."
>
> I explained what the Bible said about Christ coming the first time, dying on the Cross, rising from the dead, and then promising that He would come back again. "Only then," I said, "are we going to have permanent world peace."
>
> "Very interesting," he replied, looking away. "We'll have to talk more about that some day." And he drove on.
>
> Several years later, we met again, at the 1963 National Prayer Breakfast. I had the flu. After I gave my short talk, and he gave his, we walked out of the hotel to his car together, as was always our custom. At the curb, he turned to me.
>
> "Billy, could you ride back to the White House with me? I'd like to see you for a minute."
>
> "Mr President, I've got a fever," I protested. "Not only am I weak, but I don't want to give you this thing. Couldn't we wait and talk some other time?"

It was a cold, snowy day, and I was freezing as I stood there without my overcoat.

"Of course," he said graciously. (But the two would never meet again as later that year John F. Kennedy was shot dead by an assassin's bullet).

Graham comments, "His hesitation at the car door, and his request, haunt me still. What was on his mind? Should I have gone with him? It was an irrecoverable moment."

When our regrets are held under control and kept in proportion, they are not a problem to us, but for some people, the memory of a situation that created their regrets never seems to leave them. Tormented by these thoughts, they rehearse what might have happened and how things could have been different if only they'd been able to 'turn the clock back' and make an alternative choice. Those unresolved regrets then become a major difficulty hindering Christians from fulfilling their destiny.

It was Frank Sinatra who famously sang, "Regrets? I've had a few. But, then again, too few to mention...." These glib words are expressed very casually, but rarely are they as trivial as they are made to appear. In reflecting on choices we've made or not made throughout our lives, the impact our decisions have had can be quite significant, not only upon ourselves, but also our family, friends and those we've come into contact with.

What Are Regrets?

One helpful definition for this emotion is, 'Pain of mind on account of something that has happened, with a wish that it had been different; a troubled feeling over something one has done or left undone. It is a looking back with dissatisfaction, longing, grief, or sorrow, especially a mourning on account of the loss of some joy, advantage, or satisfaction.'

It would be true to say that anyone who has ever lived is able to identify with the feeling of regret at some time or other: regrets regarding choices made in the past causing them to waste time wishing they hadn't done or said certain things; regrets resulting from choices which influence their present circumstances that leave them feeling frustrated, discouraged, resentful and discontent; or regrets relating to decisions made which affect the future, resulting in feeling apprehensive regarding the unknown -

hesitant about how things might unfold and fearful of the changes that are likely to be necessary.

The experience of regret is universal because we are not perfect; we make mistakes, stumble, say foolish things and make bad decisions. This problem transcends age, gender, race, culture, religion and social status. It is something we all have to face and deal with because the power of regrets can either make or break us depending on how we handle them. Somebody once said,

> "Unresolved regret is a maximum security prison. Its iron bars are forged from our memories, our guilty consciences and our grief. Regret is not just about the past, though it often begins there. Decisions or actions you made a while back determine where you are today and limit where you will be tomorrow as you wish you had done differently or chosen an alternative path."

There are two major forms of regret common among Christians, both of which are very powerful. The first is a healthy expression of sorrow, born of the Holy Spirit, and always has a positive impact upon a person seeking to live for God. It brings sadness for mistakes that have been made, or a wrong that has occurred, but ultimately leads to change and freedom. The Bible refers to this in 2 Corinthians 7:10a, by saying, *"For godly grief produces a repentance that leads to salvation and brings no regret..."* Because it produces repentance it is always productive:
"See what earnestness this godly grief has produced in you, what eagerness to clear yourselves, what indignation, what alarm, what longing, what zeal...."
(verse 11)

An example of this was seen on the Day of Pentecost when in Acts 2:37 those listening to the preaching of Peter were, *"cut to the heart,"* when he said that they had crucified the Son of God. They deeply regretted their rejection of Christ and the part they had played in His death; this motivated them to cry out, *"What shall we do?"* Their sorrow caused them to want to change.

Another clear example is seen in the story of The Prodigal Son. Here we have a young man who felt considerable regret because of the selfish and foolish decisions he'd made. His remorse for the shame his rebellion had brought upon the family

was expressed in his decision to go back home and confess his wrongdoing. In genuine repentance he said,
> *"I will arise and go to my father and I will say to him,
> 'Father, I have sinned against heaven and before you,
> I am no longer worthy to be called your son; treat me
> as one of your hired servants.'"*   (Luke 15:18 & 19)

This regret brought about a change of mind and actions for him to return and seek forgiveness.

The second form of regret is quite different and described in the Bible as a *"... worldly grief that produces death."* (2 Corinthians 7:10b). It is a guilt that kills; a sorrow that is fatal. This is born of the flesh and seized upon by demonic powers. It has a negative, destructive and deceptive influence in people's lives bringing upon them a sense of heaviness and a spirit of despair. It leaves them feeling either disappointed with themselves, discontented about their present circumstances, depressed about their future prospects or disillusioned with other people. To be able to fulfil our destiny we must decide that we want to be released from every effect of this unhealthy influence in our lives.

Throughout the Bible we find numerous accounts of people who had good cause for feeling regret over wrong decisions they'd made. We've already looked in a previous chapter at the sin of people such as Solomon, Saul and Samson and seen that the consequences of their actions resulted in them missing their destiny. There are though, plenty of other examples in the scriptures; human frailty is laid bare so that we might learn from their mistakes:

(a) **Adam & Eve:** Although this couple was placed by God in a literal paradise, where every need was satisfied and they enjoyed a perfect relationship with their creator, a single foolish act of disobedience caused them to lose everything. Through this one reckless choice they brought upon themselves and the whole of the human race separation from God, sorrow, suffering, toil, sickness and death. What regret they must have felt as they saw how the consequences of that decision affected not only themselves, but also their children, grandchildren and the generations that followed after them.

(b) **Esau:** Here we have a man whose rash, thoughtless act in selling his birthright, brought about considerable regret. Even though he was overwhelmed with hunger, there was no excuse for him to have dealt so lightly with something so valuable. His regrets are reflected in the book of Hebrews, where we read,
> *"For you know that afterward, when he desired to inherit the blessing, he was rejected, for he found no chance to repent, though he sought it with tears."* (Hebrews 12:17)

(c) **Abraham:** This godly man had entered into a covenant with the Lord and received the most wonderful promise that he would be the father of a great nation and that his descendants would be as numerous as, *"... the stars of heaven, and as the sand which is on the seashore..."* (Genesis 22:17). When he remained childless, though, he allowed his wife to persuade him to act ahead of God's timing to make it happen himself. By sleeping with Hagar, an Egyptian servant, Ishmael was conceived and in turn the Arab people born. The consequences of that decision became troublesome to him not only in his lifetime, but are still being felt today in the conflict between the descendants of God's promise, the Jews, and Hagar's descendants, the Arabs.

(d) **Moses:** A great leader, many would say, yet he was a man who had to live with great regret. Among the mistakes he made in his life was murder, in a misguided act of defending a Hebrew slave being beaten by an Egyptian (Exodus 2:11 & 12). Also there was his disobedience in angrily striking a rock for water in the wilderness, when God had instructed him to simply tell the rock to yield its water. (Numbers 20:8-12). The consequence of this impetuous and impatient action prevented him from being able to enter the Promised Land. He'd travelled such a long way, leading the people of Israel out of Egypt, and had come through many difficult situations in the wilderness, yet one foolish act barred him from entering into God's provision. His regret over that must have been enormous.

(e) **Judas:** Perhaps the deepest and most tragic of all regrets were those felt in the heart of this faithless disciple. Jesus was not establishing his power base in Jerusalem, in the way he expected. Therefore out of greed, and perhaps frustration he betrayed his Lord with a kiss, for just thirty pieces of silver. How he must have regretted this shameful act of treachery, particularly when Jesus, in the Garden of Gethsemane, in front of those who had come to arrest Him, addressed Judas as *"friend"* (Matthew 26:50). The scripture describes this awful last scene in his life by saying,

"When Judas, who had betrayed Him, saw that Jesus was condemned, he was seized with remorse and returned the thirty silver coins to the chief priests and the elders. "I have sinned," he said, "for I have betrayed innocent blood." "What is that to us?" they replied. "That's your responsibility." So Judas threw the money into the temple and left. Then he went away and hanged himself."

(Matthew 27:3-5, NIV)

(f) **Demas:** This man was one of the travelling companions of Paul. Like Timothy and others, he was a young preacher, a kind of apprentice studying under the great apostle; someone who had tremendous potential and who could have fulfilled a significant destiny. However, Paul's disappointment in him was expressed when he said, *"For Demas, in love with this present world, has deserted me...."* (2 Timothy 4:10a). We can only imagine the regret that this one-time disciple must have felt, when looking back on that fateful decision, which led him away from his destiny into distraction and entanglement with worldly pleasures.

(g) **The Rich Young Ruler:** The sincerity of his desire to be right with God is evident in his search for assurance about the future. He turns to Christ wanting to know what he must do to inherit eternal life. This young ruler was also a man of good character and morals because he could say to Jesus that he had observed the commandments of God from his youth. The crunch came, though, when Jesus brought the challenge that if he really wanted eternal life he would have to give away his riches to the poor and follow Him. His wealth was his god and too great a price to pay, so he walked away, choosing not to obey:

> *"But when he heard this he became very sad, for he was very rich."* (Luke 18:23)

He had to live with the regret of that decision. If only the rich young ruler had made the same choice as a young missionary by the name of Jim Elliott who sacrificed everything, even his own life, to serve Christ. The outcome for him would then have been very different. Jim Elliott said, "He is no fool who gives away what he cannot keep to obtain that which he cannot lose."

In contrast to those bound by the chains of regrets, the apostle Paul, who had an enormous amount to feel ashamed of in his past, ended his days with confidence saying,

> *"I have fought the good fight, I have finished the race, I have kept the faith…."* (2 Timothy 4:7 & 8)

The regrets of his former actions were completely resolved and no longer a hindrance to him being able to fulfil his destiny. When we consider Paul's experience as he writes to the Christians in Rome, we gain some helpful insight into three specific areas of the regret that he overcame: *Firstly*, **The Personal Struggle**. *Secondly*, **The Power Of Its Effect**. *Thirdly*, **The Pathway To Freedom**:

> *"I do not understand my own actions. For I not do what I want, but I do the very thing I hate. Now if I do what I do not want, I agree that the law is good. So then it is no longer I that do it, but sin that dwells within me. For I know that nothing good dwells within me, that is, in my flesh. I can will what is right, but I cannot do it. For I do not do the good I want, but the evil I do not want is what I do. Wretched man that I am! Who will rescue me from this body of death? Thanks be to God through Jesus Christ our Lord!"*
> (Romans 7:15-25)

Firstly, **The Personal Struggle**

There is a constant battle taking place within the believer and Paul sums up this struggle when he says in verse 15, *"I do not understand my own actions. For I do not do what I want, but I do the very thing I hate."* The same conflict is mentioned again in verse 19, *"For I do not do the good I want, but the evil I do not want is what I do."* This struggle is present in every person's life in some measure, but not everyone is as honest and open as Paul about it; in fact this is probably the most transparent account we find in scripture regarding such a common problem.

We can appreciate Paul's struggle because we know only too well it is much easier to do the things that are wrong than that which is right. While not absolving himself from any personal responsibility, or making excuses for the mistakes he'd made, Paul identifies the root of this struggle in verses 17 & 20 as the sin nature within him.

A helpful illustration in this regard is seen in a game of bowls played on a perfectly flat green. The object of the game is to try and get the ball as close to the white jack at the other end of the playing area as possible. When the ball is rolled it will veer off to the right or the left; it does not and cannot run in a straight line. This is because built into the side of the ball is a bias – a weight that will send it in one direction or the other. The same is true within ourselves; it is our sin nature that causes us to drift away from the direction of God's will and make us live in a way that is contrary to the straight path of righteousness.

Again, when thinking of the effect of our sin nature we only need look at a young baby. Everyone gazing at a newborn child is drawn to comment how angelic the infant looks and what a picture of innocence they are. However, we know it isn't very long before the discovery is made that the child is no 'angel'- the sin nature it has is soon revealed! No one has to teach a child to lie - they need to be taught to tell the truth; you don't train a child to be selfish - you show them how to share; a child doesn't have to take lessons in being unkind, they must learn to love and forgive. The tendency towards sin is inbuilt. We are predisposed towards doing wrong rather than right: broken promises, careless words, foolish actions, wrong attitudes, missed opportunities, failed efforts, disappointing results, and a hundred and one other things all result in regret for not being or doing what we know we should, and they are the product of our sin nature.

These regrets can be felt in every aspect of life, maybe over something very recent or perhaps issues that go back many years. They can be found in:

(a) **Our Relationships:** This can be the case whether as a single person seeking fulfilment, approval or acceptance from others; in marriage with all its pressures and expectations; within the family as parents try to relate to rebellious children or children to 'out of touch' parents; rivalry between siblings seeking attention; conflict and misunderstandings in the wider family network; or the competitive, complex relationships with colleagues at work and even in the church.

(b) **Our Spiritual Development:** Our intention to have a closer walk with God might be completely sincere. We may genuinely be determined to have a deeper prayer life; to develop a greater hunger for reading God's Word; to be more disciplined in purity, or to have a greater passion to witness to others about Christ etc. Sometimes, though, it can be like taking one step forward and two steps back; no matter how clear our aim is we just keep falling short every time.

(c) **Our achievements:** As we look around at other people's success and compare it with our own we can feel disappointed with ourselves. Also, in looking back over the passage of time, both in terms of our education, career and ministry opportunities, we see the plans and hopes we had for the future, in our earlier years, have come to little and we're left dwelling on unfulfilled dreams and unrealised ambitions.

Though regrets can be perilous, pervasive and powerful, they are only ever a significant issue to anyone if they remain unresolved. This is something we should never allow to happen because the damage they can cause is substantial, as we shall now consider.

Secondly, **The Power Of Its Effect**

Unresolved regret creates fertile ground for demons to sow seeds of condemnation, shame, failure, despair and depression. Seeds will always grow quickly in fertile soil and result in a harvest. These seeds produce a faith that is paralysed, a potential that is imprisoned and a mind that is polluted - the ultimate outcome being a life that is frustrated and unproductive.

The immediate results of regret produce emotions that can be debilitating to a healthy life and their influence was clearly felt by the apostle Paul when he wrote to the Roman Christians. He reveals something of the damage that can be caused by the problem in just one sentence when he cries out saying,

> *"Wretched man that I am! Who will deliver me from this body of death?"* (Romans 7:24)

Here we find some of the seeds that are able to spring up and the consequences, if it were not for Christ, have the potential to produce a damaging effect in our lives:

(a) **Guilt and Condemnation:** We become preoccupied and imprisoned by the memory of the bad things we've done, or good things we have failed to do, and as a result it causes us to turn inward. Whenever we start to focus on ourselves rather than on the Lord it is always the start of our predicament appearing greater than God's power. In taking our eyes off Jesus we end up sinking into difficulty, just like Peter. Although he initially began to walk on water, in the realm of the supernatural, he became more conscious of the problems than the possibilities.

(b) **Shame:** Abject feelings about our own worth quickly develop and the view we have of our potential becomes distorted. We soon start to feel wretched about ourselves, disappointed and discontent with the way we are, and so start to think negatively about our value to God and those around us. We see ourselves only as a helpless, inadequate, fallen individual and lose sight of how scripture describes us. In listening to Paul we see his negative feelings result in negative speaking. Paul's conclusion about himself as he looked inside at his life was expressed with words of exasperation: *"O wretched man that I am!"*

(c) **Failure:** Mistakes we've made, or disappointment of not having lived a life that anywhere near matched our earlier dreams, makes us feel a failure. One of the recurring disappointments hunting us, particularly when we get into our mid 40's and beyond, is all about 'what could have been.' The self-talk going on inside our mind is littered with 'would haves/should haves/could haves.'

Consciousness of failure creates low expectations. In thinking and seeing ourselves as, 'not as good as we could have been,' we start to live that way, not expecting any different. Our confidence is eroded and living below God's best for our lives becomes the natural outcome, which is why Proverbs 23:7 says, *"For as he thinks in his heart, so he is...."* (Amp.)

(d) **Despair:** Now we sink deeper and go one step beyond the feeling of failure. Our regrets over what we have done or said, the opportunities we have missed, and the perception we have of ourselves, generates a notion, no matter how fleeting, that it is irretrievable; there is no way out, no way of changing the situation; no hope! – *"Who will deliver me from this body of death?"* These feelings of despair and hopelessness are of course far from the truth of God's Word; they are a lie from the enemy intent on blocking our destiny.

Many years ago, a young mid-western lawyer suffered from such deep despair that his friends thought it best to keep all knives and razors out of his reach. He questioned his life's calling and the prudence of even attempting to follow it through. During this time he wrote, "I am now the most miserable man living. Whether I shall ever be better I cannot tell; I awfully foresee I shall not." Miraculously, though, this God-fearing man, Abraham Lincoln, went on to fulfil his destiny, and the achievements of his life thoroughly vindicated his previous struggles with despair.

We know, therefore, if regrets are a problem to us by the effect they have upon our life. To speak about the *'Ruin'* of regrets is not too strong a word because that is exactly what they have the potential of doing. Regrets can ruin our joy, confidence, freedom, peace, victory, expectation, self-esteem and so much more. However, we are not left by God as helpless victims, on the contrary, our destiny is to be hope-filled victors in every situation!

Thirdly, The Pathway To Freedom

There are realms of earthly experience we have still to travel; depths of God's will we have never discovered and dimensions of the supernatural we have yet to experience that the Spirit of God wants to lead us into. Unresolved regret in all its varying forms and degrees consistently prevents this happening. The good news is, though, that we can find a pathway which leads us to a place of complete liberty from its grip. When Paul considered his inner conflict with this problem he answered his own question, - *"Who will deliver me from this body of death?"* - by declaring in Romans 7:25, *".... O thank God! - He will! through Jesus Christ, the anointed one, our Lord!"* (Amp.)

The gospel of Christ proclaims release to the captives, and to every person struggling with the effect of regret; the Bible tells us,

> *"For God sent the Son into the world, not to condemn the world, but that the world might be saved through Him."* (John 3:17)

Jesus came, anointed by God, to break all bondage in our lives and it is through Christ alone we find freedom. The journey along this pathway begins by understanding the truth that Paul discovered and of which he wrote:

> *"There is therefore now no condemnation to those who are in Christ Jesus. For the law of the Spirit of life in Christ Jesus has set me free from the law of sin and death."* (Romans 8:1 & 2)

Here the apostle refers to two spiritual laws that are just as real and firmly established as the natural laws of gravity and aerodynamics. The Law of Gravity, discovered by Isaac Newton, keeps us earthbound and has a strong downward pull on all of creation. However, no matter how dominant and powerful this law is, the Law of Aerodynamics is able to conquer it. Wilbur and Orville Wright, inventors and pioneers of the first aeroplane, proved this to be the case as they took to the sky in their flying machine on December 17th 1903 near Kitty Hawk, North Carolina.

When we observe an aeroplane, even though it may weigh hundreds of tons, we see that the Law of Gravity can be overcome. The plane is released into a new dimension, soaring through the air, no longer restricted, but able to achieve amazing heights and discover new horizons. In the same way, the Law of the Sprit of Life in Christ Jesus sets us free from the Law of Sin and Death. The more we live according to the 'Law,' or principles of the Spirit, the more we are liberated from the ruin of regret, to enjoy our new life in Christ Jesus. This is why Paul says,

"So you also must consider yourselves dead to sin and alive to God in Christ Jesus." (Romans 6:11)

We need to shift the focus of our attention away from ourselves, and set our hearts on spiritual principles. In Romans 8:4b we read about those, *"... who walk according to the Spirit"* and in verse 5b Paul states, *"... those who live according to the Spirit set their minds on the things of the Spirit."* There are spiritual principles that we must live our lives by if we are to fully enjoy the new dimension of life and horizons that take us beyond the bondage of regret:

(a) **Realise God Gives Us A Second Chance:** *"He does not deal with us according to our sins...."* (Psalm 103:10a). We do not receive from God what our wrongdoing deserves. Here is the initial, most basic principle that releases us into a new dimension of living; our mistakes are never final, we can receive a second chance. To benefit from this, though, we need to first look back and ascertain clearly the source of our regret; what it is that troubles us; the thing we did or didn't do. In discovering this we establish our responsibility, but also that the final word on the matter is God's and He has promised never to turn away those who earnestly seek Him.

Where consciousness of missed opportunities occupy our thoughts and we become overwhelmed by the fact of so many wasted years, we can be encouraged in God's grace as the Redeemer and Restorer of our lives. Maybe

you wasted yesterday – perhaps you've wasted all your yesterdays, but God's promise is,
> *"I will restore to you the years which the swarming locust has eaten…."* (Joel 2:25a)

(b) **Renounce All Regret By Confessing Our Sin:** Regret without confession leads to guilt and condemnation. Having admitted our responsibility we confess the mistakes we've made, rather than bury or suppress them, make excuses for what we have done, try and justify ourselves, or blame other people. True and sincere confession gives us the right before God to renounce the hold of every regret upon our lives so that we can turn our back on it, never to give it another thought.

One of New Zealand's greatest literary figures was novelist and poet Katherine Mansfield. She rose to fame in the 20th Century and was closely associated with D.H. Lawrence. She achieved the things she did because of her determination to never let regret hinder her life. She said, "Make it a rule of life never to regret and never to look back. Regret is an appalling waste of energy; you can't build on it; it is only for wallowing in."

(c) **Receive Forgiveness:** The confession of our sin is only part of the transaction; we also need to receive God's forgiveness and, where possible and appropriate, the forgiveness of others affected by our sin. We will know we have done so when we are able to fully and finally let go of the past. We can't change yesterday, only today, therefore it is essential that we gladly accept God's forgiveness, believing,
> *"There is now no condemnation for those who are in Christ Jesus."* (Romans 8:1)

In doing this we must similarly forgive ourselves, so that we stop beating ourselves up over issues we've previously brought to the cross. It is then that we can experience the joy of forgiveness that the hymn writer Horatio G. Spafford expressed so well when he said,
> "My sin, Oh, the bliss of this glorious thought!
> My sin, not in part but the whole,

Is nailed to the cross and I bear it no more,
Praise the Lord, praise the Lord O my soul!"

There is one other essential aspect of forgiveness, if we're to be released from regret, and that is to forgive anyone who has wronged us and through his or her actions brought regret into our lives. We need to let go of every wrong attitude no matter how justified we may feel it to be. The importance of this is inseparably linked to being able to know the power of God's forgiveness for our own sin and is why the Jesus said,
> *"If you do not forgive men their sins, your Father will not forgive your sins."*   (Matthew 6:15, NIV)

(d) Reject Every Accusation Of The Enemy: Regrets are certainly one of those things in our lives that the evil one effectively exploits as much as we allow him to. A major weapon he employs against the fulfilment of our destiny is accusation, and why the Bible describes him as, *"The accuser of the brethren."* (Revelation 12:10b). He delights to remind us of our shortcomings because he knows how devastating that can be. In doing this he is trying to destroy our confidence, squash our enthusiasm, and inhibit our faith.

We can, however, in Christ's authority choose to reject every accusation he brings before us in the certain knowledge that the blood of Christ has fully and completely cleansed us in God's sight. Regrets then can become our INSTRUCTOR and not our INTERROGATOR. As we learn from them and move on, our focus is not on the past, but as God's Word says, on what lies ahead:
> *"Forget the former things; do not dwell on the past. See, I am doing a new thing! Now it springs up; do you not perceive it?...."*   (Isaiah 43:18 & 19, NIV)

Living Beyond Regrets

The pathway leading away from regrets must have a destination that takes us to a life enjoyed beyond being freed from the problem; release is not an end in itself. Paul says,
> *"For freedom Christ has set us free; stand fast therefore, and do not submit again to a yoke of slavery."*   (Galatians 5:1)

In being released from the ruin of regret, and coming out of its shadow, we need to remain free so we can occupy ourselves in the pursuit of our destiny. There is a life of discovery, development and distinction that we can find but this is only experienced by taking specific, practical steps towards that end:

(a) Decide The Kind Of Person You Want To Be: Imagine being able to attend your own funeral service - being a silent un-observed witness to everything taking place. As you slip in the back door and take your seat, you see the altar is covered with flowers, the organ is playing softly, and the church is filled with people who have come to pay their last respects and give thanks for your life.

Several people have been asked to give a tribute: a family member, a good friend, a fellow worker and a church associate. They are all going to say a few words about you. Consider what kind of person you want them to say you were? What kind of husband, wife, father, or mother? What kind of friend or fellow worker? What would you like them to say about your character? Which achievements or memories would you like them to mention? Perhaps it might be, "He always had time for people." – "She never had a bad word to say about anyone." – "I've never met a person that was more dependable." – "There was no one he wouldn't help." – "He was known by everyone for his integrity."

As you look around at the people who are there, what difference would you like to have made in their lives? What will you leave behind that will count a hundred, two hundred years from now. If we want to live a life that is meaningful, worthwhile and free from regrets, now is the time to decide those things while we still have the opportunity.

(b) Dare To Dream Dreams: To achieve our destiny and continue to live free from the regrets of what might have been, we need to set goals for our lives that we can aim towards, pray into and see attained. If we are to stay in victory over regret it is important always to keep hope alive.

Before the American editor and author Norman Cousins died in November 1990, he had received hundreds of awards including the Peace Medal from the United Nations, nearly fifty honorary doctorate degrees and also served as a diplomat during three Presidential administrations. He lived an extraordinary life and wrote, "The tragedy of life is not death, rather it is what we allow to die within us while we live."

Another remarkable example is John Goddard; like most 15-year-olds he had a wealth of enthusiastic dreams. One ordinary day in 1940, he bothered to write 127 of his life dreams on a piece of paper. Most lists like that wind up in the attic or the bin. John's, though, became a blueprint for his life and today he is remembered as one of the world's most famous explorers and adventurers. The philosophy that characterized his life was, "To dare is to do, and to fear is to fail."

In 1972, Life magazine reported that, at age 47, he had achieved 103 of his original dreams. That article, entitled 'One Man's Life Of No Regrets,' detailed his master Dream List and became one of the most requested reprints in the magazines long history. His list included a vast spectrum of dreams: visiting eight world-class rivers; studying 12 primitive cultures; climbing 16 of the tallest mountains; carrying out careers in medicine and exploration; visiting every country in the world; learning to fly an airplane; riding in a blimp, balloon and glider; playing the flute and the violin; going on a Church mission; teaching a college course; living with head hunters in Borneo and New Guinea and many more.

(c) **Discipline Yourself To Make It Happen:** There is no use having dreams or goals in life unless you determine also to put some effort into seeing them come to pass. It will take discipline, and the temptation will always be to keep putting it off till a later occasion. Though hard work will be involved, the results will be worthwhile. Therefore, if you want to be remembered as a generous person, then start giving today. If you want people to look back and think of you as a considerate person, then start taking steps to go out of your way and show consideration to someone today. If you want to be thought of as a kind person, today is the time to start being kind. Don't put it off a moment longer because you may leave it too late!

I remember very clearly, in my early years as a teenager, the fulfilment and achievement I felt at becoming a champion boxer. Although I was knocked out in my first ever bout, through training and gruelling hard work four nights a week, in the gym and out doors in the cold and rain, I went on to succeed. Self-discipline and personal sacrifice to reach the level required was an essential part of that pathway to victory. It could not be left till 'another day,' regardless of the weather conditions or any personal comfort. In the Christian life this is even more important if we are to fulfil our dreams and is why the apostle Paul said:

"But (like a boxer) I buffet my body - handle it roughly, discipline it by hardships – and subdue it, for fear that after proclaiming to others the gospel and things pertaining to it, I myself should become unfit….." (1 Corinthians 9:27, Amp.)

(d) Walk By Faith Not Feelings: Faith in God's everlasting love, His sovereign purpose and His almighty power are the sources of our strength. As we occupy ourselves with what lies ahead, rather than dwell on the past, we must refuse to allow the negative feelings of 'what might have been' to affect us. Alexander Graham Bell, inventor of the telephone, once said, "When one door closes another door opens; but we so often look so long and so regretfully at the closed door, that we do not see the ones which open for us."

Our faith will enable us to carry on when our feelings would tell us to give up. Regardless of the amount of doors that may close in our face, the size of the obstacles that stands before us, or the personal limitations we may feel we have, when we believe in something we need to persevere.

Christopher Reeve, in his book, 'Still Me,' talks about playing Superman, and the glib definition he used to have of what a hero was. In those days, he said: "A hero is someone who commits a courageous action without considering the consequences." But since the accident that has left him paralysed, he has changed it to: "A hero is an ordinary individual who finds the strength to persevere and endure in spite of overwhelming obstacles."

(e) See Eternal Significance In All You Do: In the simplest things we do there is great importance. The key to maintaining a life without regrets is to live today like it matters for eternity – because it does! If we want to continue living free from regrets we must see there are no 'throw-away' moments, every day matters. We must look for eternal significance in our work, our words and our relationships; recognising the eternal value of the little things we do.

A young woman, who had recently lost her husband, told the story of when she and her family were having Thanksgiving Dinner and everyone was saying what they were thankful for. Her eight year old son shared, "I'm thankful for the days that Dad went outside and played ball with me." The woman said, "My husband's office was at home and whenever a client missed an appointment, he would take Michael outside and they'd play ball together. He did it to defuse his anger over the client missing a session; he had no idea he was creating a memory that would last a lifetime." Then she said, "If he had realised how significant it was, I'm sure he would have done it more often."

We need a divine perspective on whatever we do so that we see the 'bigger picture' and understand the importance of what it is we are toiling for. Just like the three workmen who were asked by someone one day what it was they were doing: the first said, "I'm laying bricks." The second said, "I'm making £9 an hour." The Third responded, "I'm building a Church for the glory of God." All three were working at the same job, but each had a different perspective about it. Every day matters; there can be eternal significance in the smallest, most mundane of things.

(f) Understand Nothing Done For God Is Wasted:
Sometimes it might appear that our plans have come to little and we haven't achieved what we set out to do. Our dreams might have been great and our intentions carried through with hard work, yet what we expected to accomplish seems unfinished. In such situations there is a temptation to slip back into a feeling of regret and think that our time and efforts have been meaningless. The reality is, though - no work done in faith for God's glory is ever wasted.

In 1904 a child of wealth, William Borden, heir to the Borden Dairy Estate, graduated from a Chicago high school a millionaire. To celebrate, his parents gave him a trip around the world. As he travelled through Asia, the Middle East, and Europe it gave him a burden for the world's hurting people. Writing home, he said, "I'm going to give my life to prepare for the mission field." When he made this decision, he wrote in the back of his Bible two words, 'No Reserves.' Turning down high paying job offers after graduation from Yale University, he entered two more words in his Bible: 'No Retreats.' Then after completing studies at Princeton Seminary, he sailed for China to work with Muslims, stopping first at Egypt for some preparation. While there he was stricken with cerebral meningitis and died within a month. A waste, some might say! Not in God's plan. In his Bible, underneath the words 'No Reserves' and 'No Retreats,' he had written the words, 'No Regrets.'

In conclusion: we all have regrets about a whole variety of different things we've said, done, or omitted to do. We must refuse to let them ruin our lives and destiny. They should never be left unresolved or allowed to be a dominant influence; instead we can learn from them and let the Lord bring change in us through them. It is God's will for every person, not only to be released from the ruin of regret, but also to maintain that life of liberty as they make the choice to:

Firstly   -   **Admit The Personal Struggle.**

Secondly   -   **Acknowledge The Power Of Its Effect.**

Thirdly   -   **Advance Along The Pathway To Freedom.**

Chapter 7

Choosing To Trust In The Power Of The Blood

You Are So Much More Than You Have Become! If someone said this about a newborn baby, held proudly in its mother's arms, it would be self-evident. Also when observing a young child, the same comment would draw equal agreement. Even looking at the rebellious, strong-willed teenager, we could recognise the unrealised potential and confidently say, "He is more than he has become!" This same assertion is also true, though, for every adult, whatever age they might be, and it is essential for us to believe if we are to see our destiny fulfilled. The revelation of this to our hearts stops us settling down, accepting a mediocre life, and it stirs us up to realise all that God has planned for us to be.

The truth of God's Word is given to each one of us so that we can develop beyond the limits of the ordinary and move into the realm of the extraordinary, doing great exploits for the Lord; this is why Jesus said,

> *"You will know the truth and the truth will make you free."* (John 8:32)

This liberating power pertains to every aspect of God's Word, but probably none more so than the truth concerning the power of the blood. Even though it is without doubt one of the great mysteries in the Bible, when we *'know'* the reality of it, then a life-changing force is discovered by all who believe.

Very few sermons are preached on this subject today and even fewer books written. Recently, while visiting a large Christian bookshop in the north, I enquired what titles they had about 'The Blood of Christ'. There were numerous books on Faith, Healing, Revival, Prosperity, Deliverance, Counselling etc., but out of their entire stock, which was considerable, there was only one book that could be found on 'The Power of The Blood.' This is no coincidence, because one of the cunning tactics of Satan is to distract people away from that which could be of the greatest importance to them. He pushes into the background of people's minds anything that is threatening to himself and whatever is most likely to cause people to see their destiny realised.

The old hymn, written by Lewis E. Jones in 1899, states: *"There is power, power, wonder-working power in the precious blood of the lamb!"* Now I know the words, *"Wonder-working Power!"* sound a bit like a 'glitzy' American advert, but it is nevertheless true. The Power of The Blood is able to bring: (a) Forgiveness for every sin, (b) Healing for every sickness, (c) Deliverance from every bondage and (d) Victory for every defeat! Therefore it is vitally important that we fully appreciate what it can accomplish in our lives.

It would be true to say that there is no other scriptural idea from Genesis to Revelation more consistently and more prominently kept in view than the power of the blood to God. While we might not fully understand it, we can be sure He certainly does. Right throughout scripture God has no other way of dealing with sin, no other way of bringing mankind into a meaningful relationship with Himself and no other way of guaranteeing His promises than through our faith in the power of the blood. This great mystery is spoken of in Hebrews 9:11-22, where we find 10 times in 12 verses the blood is referred to:

> *"When Christ appeared as a high priest of the good things that have come, then through the greater and more perfect tent (not made with hands, that is, not of this creation) He entered once for all into the Holy Place, taking not the blood of goats and calves, but His own blood, thus securing an eternal redemption. For if the sprinkling of defile persons with the blood of goats and bulls and with the ashes of a heifer sanctifies for the purification of the flesh, how much more shall the blood of Christ, who through the eternal Spirit offered Himself without blemish to God, purify your conscience from dead works to serve the living God. Therefore He is the mediator of a new covenant, so that those who are called may receive the promised eternal inheritance, since a death has occurred which redeems them from the transgressions under the first covenant. For where a will is involved, the death of the one who made it must be established. For a will*

> takes effect only at death, since it is not in force as long as the one who made it is alive. Hence even the first covenant was not ratified without blood. For when every commandment of the law had been declared by Moses to all the people, he took the blood of calves and goats, with water and scarlet wool and hyssop, and sprinkled both the book itself and all the people, saying, 'This is the blood of the covenant which God commanded.' And in the same way he sprinkled with the blood both the tent and all the vessels used in worship. Indeed, under the law almost everything is purified with blood, and without the shedding of blood there is no forgiveness of sins."

There are many things that we don't fully comprehend in life, yet we still benefit from them. For example: with the radio we cannot see any of the transmitted waves and we'll never be able to point to the frequency of a particular station and say, "That's Radio 4", and "Over there is Radio 2", but we still believe in them! Also with the television, we don't understand how it can produce coloured, moving pictures with sound. However, as we put our faith in what is necessary for us to do to see it operating, then we benefit from it. Again this can be said regarding the amazing development of the World Wide Web and our personal access via computers to the Internet. Very few people understand completely the full complex details of how it works, but as we follow certain principles and put our faith in them, then our lives are opened to a new and amazing world of communication and information.

The same is true with the power of the blood; we may not fully comprehend it, grasping every implication of what it means, but if we will put OUR faith in what God sees, what He has provided, what He responds to, and what He honours – then it works! A remarkable, supernatural power is released into our lives. One of the most important principles of faith for us to live by is found in Proverbs 3:5:

> "Trust in the Lord with all your heart, and do not rely on your own insight."

All that we have to do is believe God, and as with the baffling advancement of modern technology, trust what we have been reliably told and have faith in what has been proven by millions to work, then it will change our lives!

The Purpose Of The Blood In The Old Testament

Because of God's Holiness He established that the only way sin could be forgiven and a person approach Him in worship was through the sacrifice and shedding of animals' blood. This is why we read page after page throughout the Old Testament of rams, lambs, bulls and birds being offered in sacrifice. The regular slaying of these animals must have been a gruesome sight and it would seem that blood was everywhere, but as morbid as it might sound there was a significant reason for this. Their death and shed blood had a threefold purpose:

(1) It was a constant reminder to the people of Israel of the seriousness of their sin and the cost of forgiveness. Certainly one of the things often absent in the Church today is a genuine awareness of how serious sin is. Once we lose sight of the blood this inevitably happens and compromise comes in. Imagine though, if every time we sinned we had to take hold of a live animal, plunge a knife into its flesh to kill it and shed its blood, this would certainly bring home to us the gravity of any wrongdoing on our part.

(2) It was a symbolic act; something that was to be representative of an innocent, substitute life being given in place of the guilty sinner. The animal that had done no wrong, had no blemish and had caused no harm was slain so that the offender might be forgiven and live. Such dramatic action gave an opportunity to express obedience and faith in God's provision to maintain a right relationship with Him.

(3) It was also a prophetic act, one that spoke of an event that was yet to take place, a sign of something that was to be more substantial and complete. Each time an animal was killed and their innocent blood was shed, it was pointing forward to the fulfilment of prophecy when Jesus Christ Himself, the perfect sacrifice, would come as, *"... the Lamb*

slain from the foundation of the world." (Revelation 13:8b, AV). He would not merely cover sin, but take sin away.

The Prominence Of The Blood In The Old Testament

Throughout the Old Testament the prominence of the blood is unmistakable. References to its 'first occurrences' are particularly important, having great significance in laying a foundation for the role that the blood was to play in the New Testament and in the life of every believer:

(a) **The First Act Of Sin:** In Genesis 3 we find that the moment mankind's relationship with God was broken by their sin of disobedience, immediately the significance of the blood was introduced. As a result of Adam and Eve's rebellion, their innocence before a Holy God was lost and they were left with guilt, shame and fear. They tried to cover the consequences of their sin by sewing fig leaves together to hide their nakedness, and in doing so man's helplessness to remedy his own problems was glaringly seen. The covering of sin by any man-made idea was never to be God's way; instead we read in verse 21,

"And the Lord God made for Adam and his wife garments of skins, and clothed them."

Right from the beginning an animal had to be slain and its blood shed so that man's sin could be covered.

(b) **The First Act Of Worship:** The account of two twin brothers, Cain and Abel, offering their worship to God has always been a great puzzle to many people:

"...Cain brought to the Lord an offering of the fruit of the ground, and Abel brought of the firstlings of his flock and of their fat portions. And the Lord had regard for Abel and his offering, but for Cain and his offering He had no regard...." (Genesis 4:3-5)

For God to reject the one and accept the other seemed very unreasonable of Him, especially when they both appeared to be equally sincere. However, when we view this in the context of how important the blood was to God it begins to make more sense.

Although Cain knew better he did not approach God on the basis of the shed blood, rather he offered to God the fruit of the ground and in doing so was giving to the Lord the product of his own toil and hard work; the evidence of his own labour. We can never make any approach to God in worship on the basis of what we have done, or in the merit of our own good works. It is only as we come, like Abel, on the basis of faith in the shed blood that our worship is acceptable to the Lord.

(c) **The First Recorded Act Of Noah:** In the account of the flood, Noah and his family were kept safe in the ark for forty days and nights. When the storm eventually abated and the vessel came to rest on dry ground they stepped out into a world that had been dramatically changed. This was an extremely important moment for mankind; a new opportunity for God and man to begin again. Therefore, the first thing that Noah did was of great significance. To mark this fresh start we read that he built an altar, took animals and birds without blemish, and then sacrificed them to God by shedding their blood. (Genesis 8:20)

(d) **The First Passover:** The Jewish people continue to celebrate to this day, 'The Passover Meal,' which is an annual event held in each Jewish household. It is still one of the most important dates in the Jewish calendar and goes back over 3,000 years. It is a commemoration of Israel's deliverance and exodus from the dominion of Pharaoh as slaves in Egypt and is referred to in Exodus 12:3-13.

This speaks of God's final judgement on Pharaoh when the plague of death came upon the first born of every Egyptian male. Deliverance was promised and protection guaranteed for the Jewish people, if, every man took a lamb, without blemish, one for each household and sacrificed it, putting the blood on the doorposts and lintel of each house. God assured them of their complete protection in verse 13b by saying,

"... when I see the blood, I will pass over you, and no plague shall fall upon you to destroy you, when I smite the land of Egypt."

(e) The First Time The Law Was Given: This is referred to in Hebrews chapter 9. Here the importance of the law was presented to Israel and the standard of life God required His people to live was made clear. Having done this, immediately the significance of the blood is introduced. Verse 19 tells us that after Moses had declared God's commandments he took the blood of calves and goats that had been sacrificed, then sprinkled with the blood the book of the law, the people, the tent and all the vessels used in worship. Then in verse 22 we read,

> *"Indeed, under the law almost everything is purified with blood, and without the shedding of blood there is no forgiveness of sins."*

We see therefore that throughout the Old Testament the blood had tremendous PURPOSE, PROMINENCE, and POWER! But that was all under the law; it was part of the Old Covenant, which was only a shadow of what was yet to come. When we move into the New Testament and Jesus steps into the picture, John the Baptist makes an amazing announcement. As soon as he sees Christ the first words he says are,

> *"… Behold, the Lamb of God who takes away the sin of the world!"* (John 1:29)

The Jewish listeners must have pricked up their ears to this statement. The significance of it would not have been lost on them; it would have been all too familiar because throughout their lives they had been steeped in the sacrificial system. Now, though, this man Jesus was being pointed to as the one who would take away, not just some of the people's sins, but the sins of the world!

Jesus came to bring mankind into a New Covenant; freedom from law and legalism; from rules and regulations; from fear and failure. He came to bring the blessing of a covenant of grace and liberty in the Holy Spirit. From this point on it was to be a relationship of love and not law, so that people's response would be out of desire rather than religious duty. What the New Covenant accomplished, that the Old could never achieve, was to bring people to the place of wanting to keep the commandments out of a personal and meaningful love for God.

God had promised that there would come a day when He would make a New Covenant with His people. Speaking through the prophet, Jeremiah, He said,

> "... I will put my law within them, and I will write it upon their hearts...." (Jeremiah 31:33)

Nothing could more indelibly have written God's law on people's hearts than what Jesus accomplished at Calvary's cross when He became the perfect sacrifice for sin. As He hung there, suspended between heaven and earth, having been rejected, humiliated, abused and put to such an agonizing death, Jesus did something in that act of love that would capture the hearts of even the most hardened, transforming them into new people.

Paul, the man who was once a Christ-hater and persecutor of the Christian faith, is one such example. The impact of Christ's love totally changed his life and redirected his destiny. In pondering this sacrifice he expresses his gratitude saying,

> "... I live by faith in the Son of God, who loved me and gave Himself for me." (Galatians 2:20b)

Also the apostle John recognised how the cross should draw a response from those who have been touched by the power of the blood. He writes,

> "We love Him, because He first loved us."
> (1 John 4:19, AV)

The effect of such love also changed the hearts and lives of rough, coarse, working men during the Welsh revival and is convincing evidence of what the power of the blood is able to do. As miners made their way back from the coal pits at the end of a long hard day, they would return, not cursing or sharing crude jokes, but joyfully singing with tear stains across their coal-dusted faces; throughout the valleys could be heard the sound of that great hymn, written by William Rees:

> "Here is love vast as the ocean,
> loving kindness as the flood;
> when the Prince of life, our ransom,
> shed for us His precious blood.
> Who His love will not remember?
> Who can cease to sing His praise?
> He can never be forgotten,
> throughout heaven's eternal days."

Jesus Himself speaks of this New Covenant of love, and significantly He does so at the Passover meal. After He had broken bread and explained to His disciples the meaning of this in relation to Himself, the Bible then tell us in Matthew 26:27 & 28,

> *"And He took a cup, and when He had given thanks He gave it to them, saying, 'Drink of it all of you; for this is my blood of the covenant, which is poured out for many for the forgiveness of sins."*

Therefore our covenant relationship today is no longer based on the blood of rams, lambs, bulls and birds, but on the value to God of the death and shed blood of His own dear Son.

It is important to see in Hebrews chapter 9, how the scriptures take care to exalt the blood of Jesus over the blood of animals. God's Word elevates the value of His blood so that we might be motivated to put our faith in all it can accomplish in the process of helping us to realise our destiny. This is spoken of in verse 13 & 14:

> *"For if the sprinkling of defiled persons with the blood of goats and bulls and with the ashes of a heifer sanctifies for the purification of the flesh, how much more shall the blood of Christ, who through the eternal Spirit offered Himself without blemish to God, purify your conscience from dead works to serve the living God."*

Such a statement is simply but clearly declaring that whatever animal's blood could achieve under the Old Covenant, the blood of Jesus Christ can now accomplish SO MUCH MORE through the New Covenant!

In considering then what the blood of Jesus has achieved on our behalf, let us look at the impact it should have on our lives and how it ought to transform us as we move forward to fulfil our destiny:

Firstly, The Blood Of Christ Brings Cleansing

The very thing that would distract us from our destiny, dwarf our stature in Christ and destroy God's perfect will for our lives is the power and presence of sin. This is so whether it is the foolishness of our own personal sin, the unkind and thoughtless sins of other people against us, or the general polluting effect of living in a sinful world.

The godless society in which we live shouts out values and attitudes from all directions, whether it's via newspapers and magazines, television programmes, shop windows or even the billboards as we walk through any town centre. We can so easily feel contaminated and soiled by the ungodliness that confronts us.

Eighteen months ago I couldn't drive anywhere around the country without seeing the latest Marks & Spencer's advert. On huge hoardings everywhere there was a picture of a naked woman, gazing out of a window, with her arms raised in the air and the caption boldly across the poster said, **Hallelujah!** - What blasphemy! This word in any language means Praise God! His name, in our society, is brought down to such a base, commercial level with the purpose of catching people's attention in such a crude and corrupting way.

We all need cleansing, even the greatest of Christians, and we see why more specifically in Psalm 24:3 & 4. David poses the question here,

"Who shall ascend the hill of the Lord? And who shall stand in His holy place? He who has clean hands and a pure heart, who does not lift up his soul to what is false...."

Here, this scripture reveals to us part of our destiny. We are not to lift up our soul to that which is deceptive and false, but to let God lift us up so we are living in reality. His intention is to raise our thoughts to a better place and our desires to a higher dimension. He longs for us to ascend and occupy the realm we were originally created to develop in. It is the position His Word speaks of when it talks about us being,

"raised us up with Him, and made to sit with Him in the heavenly places in Christ Jesus." (Ephesians 2:6)

The one sure thing about sin is that in all its deceptive and false ways it will always drag a person down and pull them under. It will destroy their reputation and character; tear apart their marriages, families and witness. This has happened to several friends of mine in the ministry that I have personal knowledge of; they have been dragged down by the power of sin and ruined.

There are times in all of our lives when we feel as though we have let God <u>down</u>, let others <u>down</u> or let ourselves <u>down</u>. It is then that we are experiencing the full gravity of sin. Also whenever we feel downcast, downtrodden and downhearted it is because of the effect of sin trying to pull us under. In contrast to this, the psalmist David appreciating God's love, praised Him saying,

"... my glory, and the lifter of my head." (Psalm 3:3b)

It is impossible for a Christian to *"ascend"* and *"stand"* in God's holy place if they feel ashamed, guilty or condemned. The Lord, however, has provided through Christ's blood not only pardon but also His great power to wash away all our sin. It removes everything that would prevent us occupying our rightful, God-ordained position. His Word assures us of this power when it says,

"... the blood of Jesus Christ, His Son cleanses us from all sin." (1 John 1:7b)

This isn't just the blatant wrongdoing that we know is clearly sinful, but also the secret and hidden sins that no one else is aware of: the motives and attitudes of our heart, the thoughts quietly occupying that private place in our minds. These as much as anything else stop us ascending and standing in God's holy place.

One great problem is that very often we don't admit our sin and therefore it remains a hindrance to our destiny. We make all sorts of excuses and rationalise what we've done. This is something we see in society today where no one will take responsibility for the damage sin causes. People blame the government, police, teachers, and parents, but until we take full responsibility for our own sin the power of the blood is unable to work in our lives. The Blood Of Christ Has Never Cleansed An Excuse Yet - and it never will! It is for this reason that the Bible says,

"If we confess our sins, He is faithful and just, and will forgive our sins and cleanse us from all unrighteousness." (1 John 1:9)

Secondly, **The Blood Of Christ Gives Confidence**

If we are certain that our lives are clean and right before God then it gives to us tremendous confidence, not in ourselves, but in what Jesus has accomplished for us. This is why the Bible says,

"Beloved, if our hearts does not condemn us, we have confidence before God." (1 John 3:21)

That is the most wonderful thing in the world to know, to be confident in the presence of a Holy God. People today are searching everywhere for confidence. One of the most common areas of need that people request prayer for in the Church is to be set free from their fears, insecurities, anxiety and feelings of inadequacy. In almost every case where people have a lack of confidence, it can be traced back to the fact that they do not have confidence before God. If they were secure in their relationship with Him they would be confident to stand before anyone or anything!

(a) **Confidence To Draw Near:** God's intention for us all is not just to lift us up to *"ascend the hill of the Lord"*, but also that we might draw near and stand in His holy place. It is not His will that we should be standing off at a distance; He longs for fellowship and intimacy. God wants us to know the wonder of friendship with Him. He is determined to restore back to Himself all that was stolen by Satan in the garden when Adam and Eve walked in unbroken intimacy and communion with Him. He longs for that level of relationship that He once knew with Moses when they were able to speak face to face as a man would speak to his friend. God seeks *"true worshippers"* who will come and draw near. The significance of the blood in this regard is seen in Ephesians 2:13:

"... You who once were far off have been brought near in the blood of Jesus Christ."

Some people feel unimportant to God; they doubt their worth, His love, and their acceptance by Him. As a consequence they don't have the assurance that they ought to. When a person's faith is in the power of the blood though, they have a confidence to come before God with boldness. This is not arrogance or presumption; rather it is knowing you are right with God and that He has made a way for you to come before Him. We don't have to bow our heads in shame, nor apologise for our presence. We are sons and daughters of the King of all heaven, the Lord of the entire universe and so we confidently draw near!

This revelation only begins to change us when we start to apply the power of the blood to our thinking and our conscience. We then discover that the same confidence the writer of the book of Hebrews had can also be ours. He said,

> *"Therefore, brethren, since we have confidence to enter the sanctuary by the blood of Jesus, ... let us draw near with a true heart in full assurance of faith, with our hearts sprinkled clean from an evil conscience...."* (Hebrews 10: 19-22)

(b) **Confidence In What He Says:** We can also have complete confidence about every promise God has ever made. In 2 Corinthians 1:20a it says, *"For all the promises of God find their Yes in Him...."* Now we may know this to be true intellectually, but it will never be a burning conviction in our heart until we have faith in the power of the blood. The important role that this should have in our experience is seen when we understand that because of the death and shed blood of Jesus, we have become beneficiaries of an incredible inheritance. We haven't got to wait until we die to receive that inheritance, but right now in life God wants us to be claiming it and living in the good of all that He has promised. This becomes clear when we read Hebrews 9:15:

> *"For this reason Christ is the mediator of a new covenant, that those who are called may receive the promised eternal inheritance...."*

It is eternal not in the sense that we have to wait till eternity to benefit from it, but in that it is passed from one generation to the next, right down throughout the centuries to ourselves, and beyond to other generations; to all who claim it for themselves.

In Hebrews 9:16 & 17, while talking about the power of the blood, the writer introduces the imagery of a will being made and the importance of establishing the death of the one who wrote it, before the will can be valid:

> *"For where a will is involved, the death of the one who made it must be established. For a will takes effect only at death, since it is not in force as long as the one who made it is alive."*

The Bible is God's last will and testament, and every promise within that will is ours to claim. It isn't a question of when *we* die, but when *Christ* died, and it is the blood that declares the death has occurred. Therefore, because the death of Jesus has been established, we are able to claim every benefit that is in His will for us.

This means we can have the same confident faith as someone like Smith Wigglesworth, who would often boldly declare, "God said it, I believe it and that settles it!" Because forgiveness is written in the will, I can claim release from guilt and judgement; it's part of the covenant. For the same reason I can claim my healing, deliverance, liberty, and the anointing. I can also claim the material provision of which His will speaks; in fact, whatever He has written and promised we can claim right away, because legally it is ours!

(c) **Confidence About Our Victory Over Satan:** We can be one hundred per cent sure about God's purpose for us to live in victory; it is part of our destiny. His Word says we are to, *".... reign in life through the one man Jesus Christ."* (Romans 5:17b). This refers not merely to when we get to heaven, but also now. In the difficulties and pressures of our daily problems we should have dominion and overcome. The apostle John expresses the same life of victory when speaking of those who are followers of Christ,

> *"He who says he abides in Him ought to walk in the same way in which He walked."* (1 John 2:6)

This is especially true with regards to our victory over Satan. Too often the devil has victory over believers, oppressing them, putting a yoke upon them, filling them with his lies and tormenting them with his suggestions. Whenever we feel any heaviness and oppression and find ourselves beginning to listen to his whispers, we need to rise up within our spirit and start to declare the power of the blood against him. Satan is terrified of the blood because it reminds him about his downfall; it speaks about his defeat and how his power has been totally shattered. Colossians 2:15 states concerning Jesus,

> *"And having disarmed the powers and authorities, He made a public spectacle of them, triumphing over them by the cross."* (NIV)

To see the application of this in the daily life of the believer we only need to read Revelation 12:11. Here great confidence is expressed in the words,

> *"And they have conquered him by the blood of the Lamb and by the word of their testimony...."*

Part of the confession of our faith is that through the power of Christ's blood there is victory for every individual! As we keep testifying about the blood of Jesus and continue to speak out against the oppression of the enemy we reinforce in our own lives that victory which Christ has already established.

Thirdly, The Blood Of Christ Causes Celebration

The result of uninhibited celebration should be the natural consequence of knowing you have been cleansed from every sin and have a new confidence to approach God boldly. When we ascend the hill of the Lord and draw near in friendship and intimacy, the Lord doesn't want us to then be dumbstruck, but to say something as we express our thanksgiving and praise. He wants us to worship Him, to get excited, to celebrate His goodness and all that He has done on our behalf.

It never ceases to amaze me in a congregation, the people that will either not be singing at all during praise and worship, or be there with their arms folded, not entering in, unwrapping and sucking on a sweet. You can tell, to a large extent, where a person is in their relationship with God by their response in worship. It is always very revealing, not so much to God because He already knows anyway, but it reveals first of all to ourselves where we are, and secondly to Satan and all his demons. Our worship needs to come out of reality; the response of our appreciation for all that God has done. This was the understanding of Henry F. Lyte when he wrote:

> "Praise my soul the King of Heaven,
> To His feet thy tribute bring;
> Ransomed, healed, restored, forgiven,
> Who like thee His praise should sing?"

The question posed in these words is a great challenge for every Christian to reflect upon. We ought to be stirred up to exuberant, extravagant worship, for He deserves nothing less.

In the natural realm we expect to be moved and to express appreciation for great achievements. This is true whether it's at Twickenham rugby ground, Old Trafford football stadium or the Wimbledon finals on Centre Court. It would be bizarre in the extreme if at any of these events the whole crowd just sat with folded arms and simply nodded in polite approval at the best efforts of those who were taking part. Not only would it be out of place, it would be insulting to those they were supposed to be appreciating. It is just as out of place in the Church of Jesus Christ when we remain unmoved, untouched and unstirred, not responding with all our heart, mind, soul and strength. Surely also it isn't stretching our understanding to suggest that it must be offensive to the Lord as well!

Sometimes people don't respond as they should because they are self-conscious, bound and inhibited, more concerned about what others might think or say. In other cases people are not responding because their hearts have grown cold, they have lost their first love; the excitement that used to be there has gone. Whatever the cause may be, if we put our faith in the power of the blood and start to apply it to our conscience, it will release us into a new level of liberty so that we might rightly express our appreciation to God.

Every 'born again' believer has a destiny to attend and participate in the greatest celebration ever to be held; our seats are already reserved. Heaven though will be a very uncomfortable place for those who don't like too much excitement, exuberance and outward display of emotion. In Revelation chapter 5 we see that the response of people in this gathering is extremely enthusiastic. Their excitement is not because of the quality of the music group, the charisma of the worship leader, or the eloquence of the preacher. The basis of their elation is **The Blood of Jesus Christ!** Verse 9-14 says:

> *"And they sang a new song, saying, "Worthy art thou to take the scroll and to open its seals, for thou was slain and by thy blood didst ransom men for God from every tribe and tongue and people and nation, and hast made them a kingdom and priests to our God, and they shall reign on earth." Then I looked, and I heard around the throne and the living creatures and the elders the voice of many angels, numbering myriads of myriads and thousands of thousands, saying with a loud voice, "Worthy is the Lamb who was slain, to receive power and wealth and wisdom and might and honour and glory and blessing." And I heard every creature in heaven and on earth and under the earth and in the sea, and all therein, saying, "To Him who sits upon the throne and to the Lamb, be blessing and honour and glory and might, for ever and ever!" And the four living creatures said, "Amen!" and the elders fell down and worshipped."*

Fourthly, **The Blood Of Christ Expects Commitment**

Commitment is an unpopular word if ever there was one. It is probably <u>the</u> most unpopular word in the Christian vocabulary - next to that of TITHING! The fact remains, though, you cannot have a true church without commitment. You can have a preaching centre, and you can have a social club, but you can't have an effective church. One of the first things that happened on the day of Pentecost, when those early Pentecostals had been baptised in the Holy Spirit and began to speak in tongues, was an expression of commitment. In Acts 2:42 it says,

> *"And they devoted themselves to the Apostles teaching and fellowship, to the breaking of bread and the prayers."*

This wasn't a sense of duty for them, rather they loved to do these things; there was a passion in their hearts, they were *'devoted'* to the basics of their Christian faith.

The blood claims everyone that it cleanses and that claim is absolute. We see this when Paul says,

> *"…. You are not your own; you were bought with a price…."* (1 Corinthians 6:19 & 20)

When the blood was shed for us the full cost was paid by Jesus to redeem us back to God. In appreciating that Jesus poured out His lifeblood, that price ought to bring from us the response of gladly giving our lives to Him.

We therefore ascend the hill of the Lord, stand in His holy place, draw near in friendship and intimacy, and celebrate as we worship Him, but then at the end of it all we surrender our lives completely. This means we go from the presence of God with a commitment to give our best, be our best and do our best, for the one who gave His very best for us.

The scripture brings the example of the commitment of Jesus to challenge our own commitment in Philippians 2:5. Here Paul says, *"Have this mind among yourselves, which is yours in Christ Jesus."* Paul is saying in effect that we should think the same way Jesus thought and have the same measure of commitment He had:

> *"…who though He was in the form of God, did not count equality with God a thing to be grasped, but emptied Himself, taking the form of a servant, being born in the likeness of men. And being found in human form He humbled Himself and became obedient unto death, even death on a cross."* (verses 6-8)

We must be real, though. At times we do get discouraged; occasionally we feel disappointed because people have let us down. We can feel hurt or offended at times, especially if we think what we have done has been taken for granted and not appreciated. It's at such times we are almost tempted to give up. Whenever we begin to feel like that, the Bible reminds us of the commitment of Jesus to strengthen and encourage our resolve. It says,

> *"Consider Him who endured from sinners such hostility against Himself, so that you may not grow weary or fainthearted."* (Hebrews 12:3)

Every time we are tempted not to be our best and give our all, the Bible just says, *"Consider Him."* The power of the blood motivates our lives, even in the most difficult of circumstances, to remain faithful to the Lord.

In conclusion then, God has committed Himself to respond to those who choose to trust in the power of the blood. Even though we may not completely understand the full extent of what it means, right now we can begin to benefit from the blessing it brings into our lives. Part of our destiny is to, (a) Ascend the hill of the Lord, (b) Stand in His holy place, (c) Draw near in worship, and (d) Surrender our lives completely. All that is necessary for us to be able to do this is found in the provision of the blood of Christ. As we start to claim the power of the blood, confessing its significance and applying it to our lives, we will discover that the power of the blood:

Firstly   -   **Brings Cleansing**

Secondly   -   **Gives Confidence**

Thirdly   -   **Causes Celebration**

Fourthly   -   **Expects Commitment**

Chapter 8

Choosing To Advance In Times Of Adversity

During the mid-1860's legislation was passed in the United States that on all American currency there should be placed the inscription, *"In God We Trust."* There have been many occasions throughout the history of this country when they have found great strength and comfort from such confident faith, never more so than since Tuesday September 11th, 2001. This was the day when Osama Bin Ladin and the Al-Qaeda terrorist network made their suicide plane attacks on the World Trade Centre in New York and the Pentagon in Washington. It is a date that will be remembered as one of the most shattering in the life of America. The appalling evil of that day, when citizens from 80 nations lost their lives, caused reverberations right around the world.

Adversity comes to every person in varying degrees, as we've already touched on in an earlier chapter, and this is particularly significant for the Christian with a destiny to fulfil. It is then, when everything seems to be conspiring against the realization of our future prospects, we need to choose, not merely to rest in God's sovereignty, but also resolve we will advance in the time of trouble. The words of evangelist Billy Graham on September 14th, in his address at the National Day of Prayer and Remembrance in Washington's National Cathedral, are particularly pertinent. He said:

> "If ever there was a time when we needed to turn to God in repentance and prayer it is now."

Then with the memory, fresh in everyone's minds, of the Twin Towers collapsing and crashing down to ground level he continued:

> "We have a choice to make as people and a nation. We can implode emotionally and spiritually, or we can

choose to rebuild again on a solid foundation. That foundation is our trust in God."

This decision to rise up from the ashes of adversity and start again, with foundations built on God's Word, is the key to all people everywhere who find themselves oppressed by difficult circumstances. When facing the problems and pressures of life, making the right choices enables them to survive and move beyond whatever evil may be attempting to destroy their hopes and dreams. In times of trouble we can: Slow Down, Slip Back, or Steadfastly Move Forward. God's Word instructs us to,
> "... be steadfast, immovable, always abounding in the work of the Lord..." (1 Corinthians 15:58)

Notice here that the command isn't to 'aim at being,' 'hope to be' or 'pray about being;' God just says, ***"Be"*** - this is part of our destiny, and when we bring our lives into line with His creative Word, He gives us all that is necessary to bring it to pass!

It is remarkable to think that every American today has in their pocket, wallet, handbag, or purse the declaration, ***"In God We Trust."*** This is true whether you are talking about the President living in the White House, or the poor person begging on the streets and sleeping in a cardboard box. The confidence that such an assertion expresses must be more than an inscription on a coin though, or ink on paper. It needs to be the conviction written on the hearts of those who are daily walking together with Christ and have decided to keep their faith in Him at all times. The only way any person can advance in times of adversity is when they believe:
> "Those who trust in the Lord are like Mount Zion, which cannot be moved, but abides forever." (Psalm 125:1)

America, like our own land, has drifted a long way from being a nation submitted to God's laws. Increasingly it has become a secular society, one that is secure in its own power and self-sufficient in its own prosperity. The commandments of God, to a large degree, are ignored in its Court Houses. The Supreme Court has in effect tried to legislate God out of its schools; in many States children are not allowed to read their Bibles in school, say prayers in assemblies or learn the commandments of

God in the classrooms. There are inevitable consequences to turning away from God.

Many Christians, when calamity strikes, are often eager to state that God is not the author of adversity. While this is certainly comforting to believe, I've come to realise it is only partially true and can bring a false sense of security, resulting in complacency. We cannot overlook the fact that it was God who sent the flood in Genesis chapter 6, wiping out almost the whole population of the earth. In that incident, the greatest of all catastrophes, just eight people who had put their trust in Him were saved.

In the book of Exodus, chapters 7-12, we find God was the one who sent plagues on Egypt, even to the extent that every first-born Egyptian male child was killed. The only people who were delivered were those who had acted upon His instructions and believed that the shedding and application of an animal's blood to their homes would protect them.

It was God who judged an entire generation of His own people Israel, by allowing them to die in the wilderness because of their disobedience and unbelief (Numbers 14:26-30). Also, God was the person who sent fire and brimstone upon Sodom and Gomorrah, destroying the inhabitants of those two cities. In that situation, just a handful of believers who had put their trust in His Word were saved. (Genesis 19:24 & 25)

As uncomfortable as this is to accept, it is nevertheless true; even though we may try to make it less disconcerting by thinking that when we come to the New Testament, God has in some way had a change of heart. We find, however, that His actions are consistent there also. In Acts 5:1-10 we read about the example of Ananias and his wife Sapphira who were both struck down dead by God as a direct consequence of lying to the Holy Spirit. Also, Paul told the church at Corinth, that those who were not showing reverence when taking the solemn rite of Communion, were bringing God's punishment upon themselves:

> *"For any one who eats and drinks without discerning the body eats and drinks judgement upon himself. That is why many of you are weak and ill, and some have died."* (1 Corinthians 11:29 & 30)

The Causes Of Adversity

It has to be said that the reasons for trouble in our lives can be many and varied. Suffering has always been one of life's great mysteries to which there is no easy answer. If we are to advance in adversity though it is important that we have a clearer understanding in this area. The causes for adversity could therefore be:

(a) **Sudden Misfortune:** This is where we might experience an unexpected accident, an unfortunate incident or an unpleasant illness - events that are simply part of every day life. They catch us unprepared, and if we are not careful, result in discouragement, doubt, disillusionment, despair and depression - each of which can knock us completely off the course that we have set our hearts on.

(b) **Some Error Of Judgement:** Whether because of a mistake on our part, or the error of someone else, we can suffer the consequences of an unwise or foolish decision. The wrong choice that has been made, knowingly or unknowingly, can bring the repercussions of difficulty and trouble upon us, in some cases lasting for many years.

(c) **Satanic Attack:** Adversity caused by an evil, demonically inspired assault upon our lives is certainly taught in the Bible. The clearest example of this is in the life of Job. In spite of his blameless walk before a Holy God, one calamity after another came against this remarkable man. In Job 1:8-12 we see that the source of all his adversity was the devil, trying to shake his trust in God. Such a prospect would be quite alarming if it weren't for the fact that Jesus is determined, just as He was with Peter, that we should fulfil our destiny. To this disciple the Lord said,

> "... Satan demanded to have you, that he might sift you like wheat, but I have prayed for you that your faith may not fail...." (Luke 22:31 & 32)

(d) **Sin:** The effect of sin always pulls us away from the heart of God, dragging us down from the height of fulfilling His purpose for our lives. Sin and its consequences cause much trouble and bring great pain to us personally, as well as to others around us. We have been created in the image and likeness of God to reflect His glorious standard of holiness in every one of our decisions. When we choose to sin, that likeness is not only marred but suffering also results. This is why the Bible says, *"Righteousness exalts a nation, but sin is a reproach to any people."* (Proverbs 14:34). When sin is present, its corrupting influence eventually brings a reproach, either directly or indirectly as it impinges its way into our lives.

(e) **Sovereign Judgement:** As we've already illustrated, alongside every possible cause of adversity we can think of, is the consequence of God's sovereign, protective hand being removed, and judgement falling. When we read the first chapter of Romans, the decline into depravity there is like reading one of the Sunday tabloid newspapers! Not only is there idolatry, but also this downward slope leads on to homosexuality and sexual perversion of every kind. Such degeneracy continues to this day even though the Bible's warning is clear:

"For the wrath of God is revealed from heaven against all ungodliness and wickedness of men who by their wickedness suppress the truth."

(Romans 1:18)

The Fear Of God

One of the most important characteristics missing in the Church today is the fear of God. This is for many an old fashioned concept, but to choose to have a reverence for God's Holiness and respect for His righteous standards, is a vital necessity if we are to discover the destiny the Lord has for our lives. The significance of this can be seen in King Solomon's words when he says, *"The fear of the Lord is the beginning of all wisdom...."* (Proverbs 9:10). Along the pathway to discovering our destiny we need much wisdom to make right decisions in our daily walk.

During the 18th Century there came a tremendous visitation of God across the land of America that has been recorded in history as 'The Great Awakening.' It was a period when the Holy Spirit was poured out in mighty power. This resulted not only in 'churched' people being changed, but also the 'unchurched' were gripped by an awesome fear of the Lord that dramatically brought them into salvation. It was a move of God that significantly transformed America and flowed from that nation to many other countries of the world.

During this period there was an anointed preacher by the name of Jonathan Edwards, who, in 1741, preached a memorable sermon entitled, *"Sinners In The Hands Of An Angry God."* It is well documented that as he proclaimed this message, people in his congregation came under such conviction of sin, that they would literally be tightly clutching their seats; holding on with white knuckles for fear that they might slip into the fires of hell!

Such preaching is almost unheard of today. We have in its place either liberal theology that waters down the truth of the gospel, robbing it of its power, or a proliferation of messages emphasising love, healing, prosperity, deliverance and the benefits of faith etc. This can be equally damaging because it distorts people's concept of God so that they only see Him as benevolent and eager to bless, while anything about reverence for His holiness is strangely silent.

Positive preaching, presenting the good news, is encouraging and without doubt it is what people want to hear. It is necessary to see, though, that there is nothing more positive, nor more powerful for us to have in our lives than the fear of God, and without this it is impossible to discover our true destiny.

The Valley Of Baca

Times of Adversity are referred to in Psalm 84:6 as *"the valley of Baca"* and translated in the Amplified version as, *"the valley of weeping."* It was known as a dry, arid and desolate place and was always representative of the occasions of sorrow and hardship that affect people. These experiences are common to every person, in each generation. Those dark difficult times that bring anxiety, fear, insecurity and sadness are something we all go through. The danger in this valley, because of the emotional turmoil that ensues, is that it is a period in our lives when troubles can cause us to make wrong choices which threaten our destiny, and ultimately result in us missing the wonderful purpose the Lord has for us.

Whatever the reason for our heartache, the positive message of the Bible is that we can advance in times of adversity when we see that we are just *'passing through'* the valley of weeping, rather than settling there permanently. In recognising this, then like the people in verse 6 & 7 our ordeal can be the making, rather than the breaking of us. It becomes part of God's divine process in our development to strengthen us, which is why we read,
> *"As they go though the valley of Baca,..... they go from strength to strength."*

This is only possible when we have made the choice, not to give in, but to set our hearts on advancing towards our destiny as is mentioned in verse 5b:
> *"... in whose heart are the highways to Zion."*

There are six 'qualities of spirit' that can be found in Psalm 84, which typify those who are trusting God, even when life is painful. They give strength to anyone determined to advance in times of adversity. These characteristics will be evident in a person who has made the decision not to let their difficulties distract them from their objective of pressing on:

(a) **An Appreciation Of God's Presence:** The psalmist says in verse 1&2, *"How lovely is thy dwelling place, O Lord of hosts! My soul longs, yea, faints for the courts of the Lord...."* Here we see someone who understands that their security is not in a building, a doctrine, an organisation or their wage packet, but in their relationship with God. They have a delight and longing to remain close to God. The most secure position to be in is to see the priceless value of a life lived in the Lord's presence, appreciating that,
> *"In Him we live and move and have our being."*
> (Acts 17:28)

(b) **An Attitude Of Consistent Praise:** David refers in verse 4 to an active consistent lifestyle of worship, rather than merely being 'religious' when it is convenient: *"Blessed are those who <u>dwell</u> in thy house, <u>ever singing</u> thy praise!"* There are a lot of 'fair weather' Christians in the Church today who only seem to express any sign of joy when things are going well for them. To advance in adversity takes a different quality of spirit. Whatever the circumstances and regardless of the difficulties, a person that has a consistent praising heart will always stand firm when others are sinking fast!

(c) **An Acknowledgement Of The Source Of True Strength:** Verse 5a speaks of knowing the importance of depending on God's supernatural strength to persevere instead of struggling on in our own ability: *"Blessed are the men whose strength is in thee….."* We can be competent in many things and have impressive natural abilities, but the attitude of the godly is always to live by the principle that their confidence and strength comes from the Lord's blessing and grace upholding their lives.

(d) **An Assurance Of Being Anointed:** Here we see something of David's boldness in verse 9, that as a man of anointing and destiny he was sure of attracting the attention, protection and help of God: *"Behold our shield, O God; look upon the face of thine anointed!"* Those that know they are anointed with God's Holy Spirit have no doubts concerning His protective hand, especially in times of trial. They are assured of His commitment to them - that His eye is upon them and He is mindful of their needs.

(e) **An Avoidance Of All Evil:** To hate all sin and love righteousness is a vital decision to make if we are to maintain our confidence, especially in difficult times. In verse 10b David says, *"… I would rather be a doorkeeper in the house of my God than dwell in the tents of wickedness."* This is one of the major choices that we face every day. There is nothing more likely to slow us down or halt our advance in adversity than sin. Without such an attitude we'll find that when trouble strikes, there will come nagging doubts that maybe because of some personal sin committed, we have brought the problems upon ourselves. We therefore need to, *"… lay aside every weight, and sin which clings so closely…"* (Hebrews 12:1). The decision not to entertain temptation in any way liberates us to continue pressing on.

(f) **An Awareness Of Being Blessed:** Our dependence upon God gives us the realisation that all the resources heaven provides have been given to us. This awareness kept David in a place of security and in a position to say in verse 12, *"O Lord of hosts, blessed is the man who trusts in thee!"* God is no man's debtor; we can never lose out by trusting in Him, especially when it seems hardest to do so and when we don't understand what is happening to us. From out of that reliance He causes His favour to be with us wherever we go. Even when passing through adversity we have the consciousness of His blessing and can confidently say,

"Surely goodness and mercy shall follow me all the days of my life…." (Psalm 23:6a)

These characteristics will be unmistakable in every person who is determined to fulfil their God-given destiny. Each one of them involves a decision to change the way we think and live. It would be true to say that if any of these is missing or deficient in our lives then we will struggle to become all that the Lord wants us to be. A strong, close relationship with God is fundamental if we are to overcome and develop into full maturity.

In view of the importance of this let us consider four things that we learn in adversity which help us to move forward into that stronger and closer relationship with the Lord:

Firstly,
We Are Reminded How Fragile And Fleeting Life Is

In our youth we tend to think we are invincible and so glide through life as though we are going to live forever. When age creeps up on us though, our view starts to slowly change. We not only notice how, strangely, bank managers, policemen, doctors and shop assistants etc. seem to be getting younger, also our friends and relatives gradually are passing away! Increasingly our perspective alters and we are made to consider our own mortality. It is then that we become conscious of how fragile we are and how quickly our circumstances can alter; this is never more so than when we are struck by a major crisis.

What particularly shook millions of people on September 11th was to be confronted with their own transience and the reminder of how tenuous life is. If even the most powerful nation in the world, America, was not safe, then nothing man can do, design or develop can be secure! On that awful day two of the major symbols of America's greatness were exposed as hopelessly vulnerable to attack. In New York, the twin towers of the World Trade Centre, which were symbolic of the nation's economic security and wealth, were suddenly and completely destroyed. Shortly afterwards, in Washington, the Pentagon, a symbol of America's military might and power was struck and threatened so easily that people's confidence was shaken. Time and again we have to learn the same lesson that Jeremiah the prophet challenged his complacent generation with:

"... Let not the wise man glory in his wisdom, let not the mighty man glory in his might, let not the rich man glory in his riches; but let him who glories glory in this, that he understands and knows me...."
(Jeremiah 9:23 & 24)

Such a catastrophe reminds us also that life is not only fragile, it is fleeting; so brief and over all too quickly. For myself, at 48 years of age and a grandfather, the inevitable nature of how time quickly passes is something I am all too aware of. I find myself frequently wondering where all the years have gone. It only seems like yesterday I was running around in my grey school shorts and kicking a ball around the playground! We only have one life; it is so precious, as James tells us,

"... For you are a mist that appears for a little time and then vanishes."   (James 4:14b)

Those hundreds of people boarding the planes that were to be hijacked on September 11th and the several thousand workers setting out to work in the World Trade Centre on that fateful morning had no idea that it was going to be their last day; that they would never return home to their families again. This is why the Bible says, *"Do not boast about tomorrow, for you don't know what a day may bring forth."* (Proverbs 27:1). The only thing we can be absolutely sure about is the present moment right now, which is why we need to make the most of every opportunity.

It may sound a morbid thought, but it is nevertheless true, you can visit any cemetery in any city and you will find your age engraved on one of those tombstones. This is a fact, whether you are six or ninety-six. Therefore the fragile and fleeting nature of our lives should compel us to live taking nothing for granted, but wanting to make right choices in all that we do.

Secondly,
We Re-assess Our Values And Our Priorities

When adversity strikes it breaks right through the barriers of secular thinking, sophisticated advances and the security of material comfort. Being confronted with a crisis causes us to re-examine the things that really do matter in life. It is then that striving for success, position, fame and prosperity suddenly seem very hollow and meaningless.

Soon after September 11th, as reporters were chasing around trying to get as much feed-back and news on how the American people were being affected by what was happening to them, one journalist interviewed a top sportsman. All the sporting events of that weekend had been cancelled and the reporter asked how he felt about this. His response was, "I don't want to play anyway; I just want to be home with my family." Also, a businesswoman, who had her business completely wiped out through the disaster, was asked to comment about how she felt. Her reply was to say, "It's not important; I'm not interested in making money anymore."

This realisation of what is important is often heard in tragic news reports from those whose homes have been destroyed by fire, earthquake, tornado or flood etc. It is common to hear them saying something like, "We have lost everything, but thank God we still have our lives!" Sometimes it takes trouble to call us back to a sense of true values, the things that really do matter in life like: love, peace, hope, friendship, health and family. This reality was experienced by restauranteurs in America, who following September 11th reported an increase in trade, simply because more people were eating out as families.

Tragedy transforms our values. One of the pupils that escaped the appalling Columbine High School massacre in Littleton,

Colorado on April 20th 1999, where twelve students and one teacher were shot dead expressed this. She was asked to say something at the memorial service shortly after the traumatic event. Her powerful words made a considerable impact on all who heard them and showed remarkable insight regarding the decline of values that has polluted every aspect of modern day life. She said:

> "The paradox of this age is that we have more conveniences, but less time, more degrees, but less common sense, more knowledge, but less judgement, more experts, but fewer solutions.
>
> We have increased our possessions, but reduced our values. We have learned how to make a living, but not a life. We have been to the moon, but still we don't know our next-door neighbour. We have conquered outer-space, but not inner-space. We have cleaned up our air, but polluted our souls ...."

In times of adversity, as we reflect on our values, it motivates us to change the priorities we have so that we radically alter the things we spend our lives pursuing. The way we spend our time, energy, and resources is very important if we are seriously concerned about fulfilling our destiny. This is why the Bible gives us a helpful warning in saying,

> *"Look carefully then how you walk, not as unwise men but as wise, making the most of the time, because the days are evil."* (Ephesians 5:15 & 16)

Time is so precious and when it is suddenly snatched away our chance then has gone to do something about those things that are really important: the phone calls to loved ones we never got round to making; the letters we always planned to write; the people we meant to spend more time with and those words we always intended to say, yet never found the courage. When adversity strikes we realise the need to do something, while we can, before the opportunity is gone!

Thirdly, **We Reach Out Beyond Ourselves To God**

One of the things that made a deep impression on me in all the coverage of events following September 11th, was the memorial service held at St. Paul's Cathedral, in London. There under one roof you had the good and the great gathered together: Royalty, Presidents, Prime Ministers, Politicians, Business Executives, and the ordinary man in the street, all standing on level ground before Almighty God; each one made aware of their personal need to reach out to their Creator for comfort and reassurance.

On the American news programme CNN, reporter Judy Woodruff said on live television, "At times like these you want to reach out to a higher being for salvation." It is in the day of trouble we are reminded of our need of God. This is why, as someone once said, **"The Seed To Your Greatest Power Is Often Found At The Heart Of Your Worst Problem."**

Sometimes God allows the worst of problems in our lives to bring us to the place of being dependent on Him, so that we don't stray away from our destiny by becoming too confident in ourselves. The apostle Paul certainly realised the wisdom and love of God in this respect and he could relate to this understanding of adversity when he said,

"For we do not want you to be ignorant, brethren, of the affliction we experienced in Asia; for we were so utterly, unbearably crushed that we despaired of life itself. Why, we felt that we had received the sentence of death; but that was to make us rely not on ourselves but on God who raises the dead; He delivered us from so deadly a peril, and He will deliver us; on Him we have set our hope that He will deliver us again."
(2 Corinthians 1:8-10)

In the summer of 2001, Foot and Mouth disease was at its height, bringing a national crisis to this country, devastating the farming community and the tourist trade. At that time Dr. Ian Paisley stood up in the House of Commons and proposed that the Prime Minster called for a national day of prayer. Tony Blair shrugged off this request and he responded by saying, "There is no need for that; people will pray in their own way." Regrettably this was a missed opportunity for people throughout our nation to collectively reach out to God and it expressed a blatant indifference to any spiritual need.

In glaring contrast to such pride the proclamation of Abraham Lincoln, spoken in 1863, at a time of national crisis during the Civil War, is quite different. He proclaimed a national day of prayer and thanksgiving with these remarkable words:

"It is the duty of nations as well as of men to own their dependence on the overruling power of God; to confess their sins and transgressions in humble sorrow, yet with assured hope that genuine repentance will lead to mercy and pardon; and to recognise the sublime truth, announced in the Holy Scriptures and proven by all history, that those nations are blessed whose God is the Lord.

We know that by His divine law, nations, like individuals, are subjected to punishments and chastisements in this world. May we not justly fear that the awful calamity of civil war, which now desolates the land, may be punishment inflicted upon us for our presumptuous sins, to the needful end of our national reformation as a whole people?

We have been the recipients of the choicest bounties of heaven; we have been preserved these many years in peace and prosperity; we have grown in numbers, wealth and power as no other nation has ever grown, but we have forgotten God.

We have forgotten the gracious hand, which preserved us in peace and multiplied and enriched and strengthened us, and we have vainly imagined, in the deceitfulness of our hearts, that all these blessings were produced by some superior wisdom and virtue of our own. Intoxicated with unbroken success, we have become too self-sufficient to feel the necessity of redeeming and preserving grace, too proud to pray to the God that made us.

It has seemed to me fit and proper that God should be solemnly, reverently, and gratefully acknowledged, as with one heart and one voice, by the whole of the American people. I do therefore invite my fellow citizens in every part of the United States, and also those who are at sea and those who are sojourning in foreign lands, to set apart and observe the last Thursday of November as a day of Thanksgiving and praise to our beneficent Father who dwelleth in the heavens."

Amongst all the saturation of media coverage on September 11th many images come to mind; one of the most dramatic was when the twin towers came crumbling down and we saw people frantically fleeing for their lives. As huge clouds of smoke and debris came crashing along the streets behind them, people were desperately trying to find a place of safety in nearby shops and under parked cars. It brought a vivid picture of the terror of insecurity and the helplessness of mankind when facing imminent danger. The confidence we have, though, as Christians, especially when evil is trying to destroy God's purpose for our lives, is found in the words of David:

> "God is our refuge and strength, a very present help in trouble. Therefore we will not fear though the earth should change, though the mountains shake in the heart of the sea; though its waters roar and foam, though the mountains tremble with its tumult."
>
> (Psalm 46:1-3)

Close to where the World Trade Centre collapsed in Manhattan, there stands a small church by the name of St. Paul's. Previously, it was dwarfed by the enormous buildings nearby, and almost unnoticed by those rushing about in their busy everyday lives. Following the disaster, though, and amongst all the rubble and ruins, that church stood intact. It became a sanctuary for the aid and rescue workers; a place of safety and quiet reflection, as well as a symbol of the security we have in God. Looking at such an image brings to mind the scripture, which says,

> "Therefore let us be grateful for receiving a kingdom that cannot be shaken, and thus let us offer to God acceptable worship, with reverence and awe; for our God is a consuming fire."   (Hebrews12: 28 & 29)

We are part of a kingdom that cannot be shaken. Our appreciation of that fact should not only, as this verse suggests, change our lives and affect our worship, it should also make us want to pass on such a glorious message of hope to those we meet.

Fourthly,
We Respond By Bringing Hope And Help To Others

To know the security and peace that comes from trusting in God places us in a position of great privilege, but also great responsibility. Our destiny doesn't end in finding this blessing for ourselves; it is never complete until we have made the choice to pour out our lives for others. This is why we read in Psalm 37:3,

"*Trust in the Lord,* **and do good**; *so you will dwell in the land, and enjoy security."*

In times of comfort and ease we can easily become self-reliant, self-absorbed, and very insular. When adversity strikes though, particularly on a large scale, and so many stand in need, invariably there is a rallying round to help those who are suffering. The British have often referred to this as the *'Dunkirk Spirit'*, but such a conclusion is a very shallow understanding of what is really happening. There is no such thing as the *'Dunkirk Spirit,'* rather; it is the presence of God's Spirit at work in adversity, even through unconverted people.

Imagine a world where there was no goodness, compassion, thoughtfulness, kindness love etc.; that would surely be an awful place. Yet we find that even in our fallen world today, no matter how evil and dark things are, still there is a measure of good. This is because God's Spirit is present among us, from which these divine and precious qualities emanate. If, however, God were to completely withdraw His Spirit, we would have hell on earth!

One of the most common questions people have asked since September 11th has been, "Where was God on that day when so many thousands lost their lives?" Our answer needs to be confident and clear: God was not in the cockpit of the two planes that were deliberately crashed into the World Trade centre and the Pentagon. He was in the fireman's suit, and behind the policeman's badge; He was with the nurses holding the bandages and syringes, and alongside the surgeon skilfully using the scalpel. God was with the rescue workers who, with all their strength and efforts, were tirelessly working under the most appalling conditions to reach those in need.

The point is that God works through people to achieve change, bringing hope and help to others, even through those who have no idea that it is Him who is doing so. This is especially true, of course, for the Church that has a calling to be the means of bringing healing to the nations. Also, for individual Christians through whom He wants to work that they might be *"The salt of the earth"* and *"The light of the world."* We are His hands and feet, His voice and His love. For this reason our desire needs to be the same as the words expressed in that wonderful hymn, written in 1874, by Francis Havergal:

> "Take my life, and let it be
> consecrated Lord to Thee;
> Take my moments and my days;
> let them flow in ceaseless praise.
> Take my hands, and let them move
> at the impulse of thy love.
> Take my feet, and let them be
> swift and beautiful for thee."

From what we have experienced of God's goodness, you and I are to be a channel of His grace to others. Paul understood this when he said in 2 Corinthians 1:3 & 4,

> *"Blessed be the God and Father of our Lord Jesus Christ, the Father of mercies and God of all comfort, who comforts us in our affliction, so that we may be able to comfort those who are in any affliction, with the comfort with which we ourselves are comforted by God."*

It is because of His presence at work within us that in times of adversity we discover:

(a) A Compassion That Is Supernatural;
(b) A Compelling Motivation To Do Something Practical;
(c) A Confidence That We Can Make A Difference!

As we share the Good News of the gospel we must take care that we are not simply preaching words, but also are demonstrating the love of Christ in deeds that are meaningful and relevant. There are many damaged and suffering people all around us in life today, especially on our own doorstep. Sin and its consequences affect the whole of mankind but we have a gospel of hope and healing, security and peace, joy and liberty to make known to others. God's call to His church at this time, and His expectation that we can make a difference is found in Isaiah 60:1 & 2:

> *"Arise, shine; for your light has come, and the glory of the Lord has risen upon you. For behold, darkness*

shall cover the earth, and thick darkness the peoples; but the Lord will arise upon you, and His glory shall be seen upon you."

God Will Always Have The Final Word

We should be the most positive and optimistic people on the face of the earth, the reason being because we have read the end of the book! We know how it is going to turn out!! Regardless of how dark the darkness gets, or how evil the evil grows, the Bible says,

> *"... But where sin increased, grace increased all the more."* (Romans 5:20b, NIV)

God is still on the throne and nothing will ever take Him by surprise! The devil thought he would have the final word on September 11th, just like he thought he had done when Jesus was cruelly nailed to the cross; he could not have been more wrong! Good emerged out of the evil of that dark day in America's history, and though the initial impact since then has regrettably diminished with the passage of time, at least we were given a glimpse as to what was possible.

After the shock and realisation of what happened then, the nations of the world came together like never before. In the immediate aftermath of the tragedy more people began to attend church than prior to that awful day, and Bible sales increased significantly following the disaster. The material security, that people for so long had put their confidence in, was stripped away, and suddenly they were made to see the importance of spiritual issues and eternal values.

It demonstrated to us that even when life appears very grim, the greatest of tragedies can be turned around and such shaking can be the preparation, not just in America, but also in this nation of ours for revival to sweep across the land. Ultimately evil will never triumph over us because our destiny is in God. This is why the positive message of His Word tells us,

> *"In the day of great slaughter, when the towers fall, streams of water will flow on every high mountain and every lofty hill."* (Isaiah 30:25, NIV)

When we read Psalm 84 against this background it begins to make more sense. There is a phrase in verse 6, which at first seems strange and hard to understand. However, when it is taken in the context of our destiny and the difference God wants our lives to make, it becomes clearer. This verse says,

> *"As they go through the valley of Baca they make it a place of **springs; the early rain also covers it with pools.**"*

What we notice from this is that hard and desolate circumstances do not adversely change those whose trust is in the Lord. Instead the people of God change the atmosphere of their environment and the circumstances around them. Revival is the ultimate objective on God's agenda. This is where we are advancing towards in our destiny and what we shall be considering in the next and final chapter.

In conclusion: with trouble all around and with a destiny for each of us to fulfil, we need to examine if we are, Slowing Down, Slipping Back, or Steadfastly Moving Forward. We can choose to advance in times of adversity, but it will only be possible when we have a strong, close relationship with God. This begins to develop as in hard times we:

Firstly - **Remember How Fragile And Fleeting Life Is,** and therefore determine to make the most of every opportunity that each day brings.

Secondly - **Re-assess Our Values And Priorities,** so that we decide to spend our time, energy and resources pursuing things that really do matter in life.

Thirdly - **Reach Out Beyond Ourselves To God,** and depend entirely on Him in our daily lives, rather than on the passing security of material possessions.

Fourthly - **Respond By Bringing Help And Hope To Others,** so that we confidently declare and demonstrate God's love, with the assurance that we can make a difference.

Chapter 9

Choosing To Prepare For Revival

In 1932, revival came to north China in answer to several years of prayer. At one point, Norwegian missionary Maria Monsen wondered what good her praying could do. She longed to see God's river of life flood spiritually dry China. Then she was reminded that the mighty Yangtze River began when tiny drops of rain came together in the top of the mountains. Maria sought a prayer partner who would join her in claiming the promise of Jesus that, *"... if two of you agree on earth about anything they ask, it will be done for them by my Father in heaven."* (Matthew 18:19). When she finally found someone she exclaimed, "The awakening has begun! Two of us have agreed!"

In November 1930, Maria announced, "A great revival is coming soon, and it will begin in the North China Mission." In 1932 about forty Christians were meeting in a town in North China for prayer, four times a day, beginning at 5.00 a.m. When revival came, believers experienced a deep conviction of sin, and more people were born again in that region than in any previous year. One missionary estimated that 3,000 people were converted in his town alone. Pastors, missionaries and Bible teachers also testified to a deeper relationship with God than they had ever known before.

Choosing to prepare for revival is one of the most important and radical decisions we will ever make as Christians. All that has been written in each of the previous chapters has been to lead us to this point. The significance of our choice now, in the unfolding purposes of God for our lives, is seen in 2 Chronicles 7:14,

> *"If my people who are called by my name humble themselves, and pray and seek my face, and turn from their wicked ways, then I will hear from heaven, and will forgive their sin and heal their land."*

God in effect is saying here, *"I will, if you will."* We can choose to let the darkness grow darker, or decide that our life, together with God, is going to make a difference. There can be little doubt that our land needs healing and there is no unwillingness on God's part to pour out His Holy Spirit and do this. However, the great mystery is that He waits for us to decide that we are ready to pay the cost and make the sacrifice required in seeing this aspect of our destiny realised.

The prospect of a brighter future and better day is not wishful thinking; rather it is the clear promise of God's Word. This is the day of which He spoke, saying,

> *"For the earth will be filled with the knowledge of the glory of the Lord, as the waters cover the sea."*
> (Habakkuk 2:14)

It is referred to in Isaiah 35:6b & 7a, when the prophet said,

> *"... For waters shall break forth in the wilderness, and streams in the desert; the burning sand shall become a pool, and the thirsty ground springs of water...."*

Also in Joel 2:28a, God declared,

> *"I will pour out my Spirit on all flesh….."*

The fulfilment of these promises is fast approaching! In the meantime though, God doesn't want you and I simply to be waiting around for something to happen. We must choose to prepare for such an out-pouring of His Holy Spirit that will change the state of decline and depravity in our nation.

In the 19th Century there lived a remarkable man of God by the name of Charles Finney. He was raised up by the Lord to bring revival into many areas. This man said: "Revival is not an accident, any more than a field of wheat is an accident!" In considering these words, it reminds us that whenever we look at a field of wheat, we see at least two things:

(a) The evidence of someone who has chosen to apply themselves to toil, labour and diligent hard work.
(b) The expression of God and man working together in perfect harmony.

This combination is what true revival involves. When God in His sovereignty and grace moves upon the lives of men, He brings an *'Awakening'*, so that there is a glad, willing, even enthusiastic desire towards Christian service. Gone is any sentiment of religious duty or feeling of obligation. Instead there is a fire burning within the hearts of those touched by God that results in a sense of awe and excitement to be involved in seeing 'His will done on earth as it is in heaven!'

We cannot plan a revival, but we certainly can decide to prepare for one. It always puzzles me when I hear of churches, particularly in America, that routinely advertise: *"REVIVAL MEETING HERE - EVERY WEEK - AT 7.30 p.m.!"* If this is an earnest intention to seek after the Lord, then He will always honour that, but usually it is just another example of man trying to organise the Holy Spirit.

While we might have our own pre-determined ideas, and would like to put God in a box of our own expectation, He is not confined or controlled by our plans. G. Campbell Morgan, who was pastor of Westminster Chapel, from 1904-1917, had the right idea when he said, "Revival cannot be organised, but we can set our sails to catch the wind from heaven when God chooses to blow upon His people once again."

The Church in Britain today has a choice that must be made: it can muddle on in mediocrity or it can have, *"ears to hear what the Spirit is saying."* I believe Christ is simply saying this to His Church: *"Revival is the heritage of our past and the only hope for our future!"* Our one hope does not rest in Politics or Economics. It is not discovered through Technology or Psychology, nor is it found in Philosophy or even in Theology. The only hope for our future is in God moving upon the hearts of people, bringing them to acknowledge that He alone is Lord!

Ezekiel 37:1-11 speaks about a promised revival. It is a vision of a valley full of dry bones, coming back to life to fulfil their original calling and destiny. One of the remarkable things about this account is how God raises up, leads step by step, and speaks through the life of one man, Ezekiel, to bring revival to a nation. Just as amazing is the way that the Lord wants to use you and me to fulfil His plans and purposes. He is quite able to do it without us; overnight He can completely change the face of this earth. However, right down throughout Church history God has always chosen to work through the frail, weak, vulnerable and foolish vessels of our lives, that He might receive all the glory.

To put this passage in context, God's servant Ezekiel has been cut off from his homeland. Judah has just been devastated as a nation, having been taken into captivity by the Babylonians. All around him there was a spiritual dryness, deadness and despondency. He was going through an extremely testing period in his life; it was a hard, discouraging and frustrating time for him.

We all, occasionally, face such seasons, maybe in our health, our finances, our relationships, or perhaps with some emotional or spiritual struggle. However, in verse 1 we find three things that Ezekiel knew which enabled him not to be overwhelmed by his difficult experience. They are the same three things that will always strengthen us to rise up from our problems and come out the other side victorious, regardless of whatever may try to defeat us. Ezekiel knew that:

(1) **The Hand Of God Was Upon Him.**
(2) **The Spirit Of The Lord Was Leading Him.**
(3) **He'd Been Placed Where He Was For A Purpose.**

We might not know very much in life, nor be that clear about many things, but if we only know these three things, they will be sufficient to see us through the hardest of times. Each one of us need to be able to say with absolute confidence: "I know that the hand of God is upon me; I know that the Spirit of the Lord is leading me; and I know I've been placed where I am - even in these difficult circumstances, for a purpose!"

In addition to this, Ezekiel was a man of vision. He could see revival coming when others around him could see nothing but hopelessness and despair. The marvellous thing about vision is: (a) it enables us to see beyond every negative circumstance of life, (b) it lifts our expectation for the miraculous, (c) it motivates our daily living with a sense of purpose, and (d) it always gives us a divine perspective on whatever may be confronting us. We should not be surprised therefore that the Bible says,

"*Where there is no vision, the people perish....*"
(Proverbs 29:18, AV)

This is not simply referring to the fact that if as Christians we have no vision for the un-churched then they will perish and go to hell. It is speaking also about the consequences on God's people, themselves. If they have no vision something dies within them spiritually; deadness creeps in whenever the Church has no clear vision.

Helen Keller was once asked, "Is anything worse than being blind?" She said, "Yes to have sight but no vision." Each one of us needs a vision of the glory and majesty of God ruling and reigning on high; a vision of His plans and purposes for such a time as this, and a vision of the part we are to play, as individuals, in those plans.

If ever there was a time when this nation and the Church needed men and women of vision it is most certainly now! How different our churches would be if only there were more people in them like Joshua and Caleb; they were men of vision. When the twelve spies went in to spy out the Promised Land, ten of those men came back with a very blurred and distorted vision. All they could see were the high walls of the city, the giants, and the obstacles in the land. As a result of this, each of them returned expressing an extremely negative confession that came out of fear, saying the task was impossible! Only Joshua and Caleb came back with a God-given vision. They could see a land *"flowing with milk and honey"* and because of this their confession of faith was:

"... We should go up and take possession of the land, for we can certainly do it."   (Numbers 13:30b, NIV)

In any church you will always find those who throughout their lives choose to see the problems and those who decide to see the possibilities. There will be some who have a negative confession of doubt and others who express a positive confession of faith. What the Lord is doing with His people today is motivating them to see beyond the **DEADNESS** of empty religion and division; beyond the **DRYNESS** of compromise and hypocrisy; and beyond the **DULLNESS** of apathy and indifference.

He is stirring His Church in these end times to rise up from its slumber and begin to move together as one in the power of the Holy Spirit. The prophetic Word of God to the Church at this time is found in Isaiah 52:1a, *"Awake, Awake, put on your strength, O Zion...."* The Lord is bringing an awakening to those who profess to believe in Christ, so that they might effectively serve Him in these last days.

As we look more closely at Ezekiel 37 let us consider four stages that are necessary in preparing for this *'day of God's Power'*, each of which requires from us a choice. We must decide to:

Firstly, Recognise Our True Condition

This is a call for personal honesty and for absolute reality. Without a daily close, personal relationship with God we remain but *"dry bones."* Whenever we are not walking in holiness, faith, obedience and unity we become *"very dry."* Revival will never come for us until we first recognise that we need it. It will always pass us by and touch someone else, move in another church or another area. Not until we first recognise that we need revival will anything truly happen.

Here in the western world, one of the great curses that the Church has brought upon itself is that of materialism. What this has done has been to make Christians comfortable, complacent and confident in themselves. We no longer have that overwhelming sense of how much we need the Lord. In contrast to this if we look at other lands, like parts of Africa, Asia and South America, places that don't have as much as we do materially, we find there that God is moving in revival power in the most outstanding way. While these people may be poor materially, they are rich spiritually because of the deep hunger and reliance upon the Lord that they have.

Therefore, in deciding to recognise our true condition we must look at verses 1 & 2 of Ezekiel's vision. As we do so we see, *"A valley full of bones,... and they were very dry."* The challenging thing is then to consider also verse 11, and find that these words are referring to the people of God:

> *"... these bones are the whole house of Israel. Behold, they say, 'Our bones are dried up, and our hope is lost; we are clean cut off.'"*

What is extraordinary is that these were God's chosen, consecrated, and covenant people. Physically they were alive; they were walking, talking, eating, working and even worshipping, but spiritually in God's sight there was:

(a) **No Dynamic Life** – What once was an impressive, fighting force was now powerless, and of no significance or threat to anyone.

(b) **No Unity Of Spirit** – They were disjointed and scattered over a wide area, and their condition made it impossible for them to function together.

(c) **No Divine Purpose** – They were motionless and very dry; all previous life was long gone and all hope was absent. No longer were they aware of any momentous destiny.

This clearly teaches us, it is not outward appearances that really matter; it is what's going on inside the heart that truly counts. The important thing is what is happening beneath the veneer of all our church activities and religious rhetoric. Revival begins when we come to the place of reality about where we are before God individually, as a Church and as a nation.

The prophet, Isaiah, was someone who had to come to this place of recognising his true condition. Before the Lord could break through in his life and release him into a ministry beyond his wildest imagining, he had to see the poverty of his own personal need. This he did when he cried out in repentance,

"Woe is me! For I am lost; for I am a man of unclean lips, and I dwell in the midst of a people of unclean lips; for my eyes have seen the King, the Lord of hosts!" (Isaiah 6:5)

The same was true for the church at Laodicea. Outwardly they looked very inspiring; in fact you'd be hard-pressed to find another church that could match these people as far as appearances were concerned. However, what God saw was quite different. He said of them in Revelation 3:17,

"For you say, I am rich, I have prospered, and I need nothing; not knowing that you are wretched, pitiable, poor, blind and naked."

We can conclude from this that it doesn't matter what we might think of ourselves, or what other people's opinion might be; the really important thing is what God sees as He searches every heart and tries every thought.

In Ezekiel 37: 9 we discover the reason for Israel's condition summed up in one word. In fact the cause of the condition in the Church today can be found there also. It is the word *"Slain."*

The picture isn't just of a valley of bones that were dead; a people who had died of natural causes, they had been slain by an enemy force; an enemy had defeated God's people!

Jesus gives us a clear warning about the power of our greatest adversary to slay. When referring to Satan He says, *"The thief comes to steal, and kill and destroy..."* (John 10:10a). Our enemy hates the Church and every disciple of Christ. He hates any thought of revival and will do everything in his considerable power to work against it. He wants to steal our opportunity of walking in intimate communion with God. His callous and calculated intention is to kill our joy, victory, peace and liberty. He would destroy the tremendous potential and God-given destiny that each one of us has.

God's people can be slain very easily through things like: pride, unbelief, immorality, fear, division, discouragement, compromise and un-forgiveness. In fact it would be true to say that every form of sin is deadly! For this reason the Bible tells us, *"... the soul that sins shall die."* (Ezekiel 18:4b). This is not talking merely about a physical death, rather it is speaking of the effect that sin has on us spiritually as it brings deadness into our relationship with God.

One of the deadliest things that can threaten our spiritual well-being is unrepented sin; where we confess our sin to the Lord, but keep on living the same way. We tell God how sorry we are about certain habits, attitudes, thoughts and reactions, but still continue to practice them. True repentance immediately lays the axe to the root of the problem and always bears the fruit of a changed life!

The apostle Paul also taught that a person who continues to live with un-spiritual attitudes or thinking would bring deadness into their own lives. When speaking to the Christians in Rome he said, *"To set the mind on the flesh is death..."* (Romans 8:6a). Notice that Paul does not speak of it *'leading to'* death, he says, it *'is'* death. If we allow the habit of such thoughts and reactions to form in our lives, rather than to live and think according to spiritual principles, then it quenches the life and vitality of our relationship with God.

Secondly, **Realise What God Is Able To Do**

Revival is never ever about bad news; it is always good news! God's Word doesn't come to condemn and crush us, nor is the intention of God to make us feel hopeless failures. The ultimate purpose of His Word is always to forgive, cleanse, release, heal, restore, renew, strengthen and transform our lives completely. This is why the question that God asks Ezekiel in chapter 37: 3 is so important for every Christian: *"Son of man, can these bones live?"* As we think about revival in our dry and barren land and in our hard and spiritually dead communities, we must be fully convinced and totally persuaded that nothing is too difficult for God. We need to choose to believe, not merely in our heads, but as a deep conviction in our hearts, that the Lord is a Supernatural, Miracle-Working, Life-Changing God!

Ephesians 3:20 tells us that God is able, *"to do far more abundantly than all that we ask or think."* He can change the unchangeable and reverse the irreversible.

One such example of this that I came across recently in ministry was a man from Ibstock in Leicester. Having listened to the preaching and heard about what God was able to do for him he made a decision to respond for prayer. This man shared with me that he had suffered with Parkinson's disease for over 10 years. We prayed together, and as a result of that night, he is now completely healed. The symptoms of shaking and slowness of speech have gone and he no longer needs any medication!

In looking at Ezekiel chapter 37, you cannot get circumstances that are more beyond hope than a valley of very dry bones. This is a situation that clearly is well beyond the possibility of change and yet it is into this desperate need that God, having said, *"Hear the word of the Lord,"* makes several amazing promises in verse 6:

> *"And I will lay sinews upon you, and will cause flesh to come upon you, and cover you with skin, and put breath in you and you shall live; and you shall know that I am the Lord."*

All God is looking for today is for people that will simply choose to believe His Word; those who will live by the conviction that He says what He means, means what He says and will do what He says He will do! To everyone facing impossible situations, Jesus declares,

"If you will believe you will see the glory of God."
(John 11:40b)

The context in which He first made this statement was certainly an impossible situation. Lazarus had been dead for four days. His body had been entombed and was even starting to decompose. We notice though that Jesus did not expect people to see the miracle of resurrection first, and then believe. He expected them first to believe, and then promised that they would see His glorious power revealed!

One of the great needs for 21st Century Christians is to rediscover their confidence in the miraculous. With the many great advances that have been made in medicine and technology today there are a variety of other things we can rely upon, other than God. Often He is not our first point of reference at a time of need.

This is particularly evident with sickness. Here in the West, when we are unwell, it is so easy for us to pick up the phone and make an appointment with the doctor, go with our prescription to the chemist or to reach for our medicine that our initial reaction is not to seek prayer, or cry out to God for a miracle. If we look at other lands though, in places where medicine isn't so available and doctors aren't so accessible, the first reaction of the Christians there when they are sick is to believe God for healing. It is little wonder, therefore, that we hear of so many wonderful miracles in other countries and not so many in our own.

Let me be clear here; I believe in the grace of God that restores the sick back to health through the skills of doctors and surgeons. The advances made in the field of medicine are part of God's mercy to deliver us from ill health. There is nothing wrong in taking medication. However, if our first reaction is to make a choice to depend on these things, rather than to respond when the opportunity is given for prayer, or to call the doctor the moment we don't feel well instead of calling out to God for healing, then that's a different matter. This kind of choice indicates that we have lost our expectancy for any divine intervention. In such instances we are fulfilling the conclusion of scripture that says,

"... You do not have, because you do not ask."
(James 4:2b)

When looking again at the question in verse 3 that Ezekiel had to face, *"...can these bones live?"*, it does bring to us a great personal challenge. Before we can answer that for our nation or our neighbourhood in terms of revival, we must realise what God is able to do about the tough situations that we are confronted with personally. The dead, dry, dull, difficult circumstances that are all around our own lives. In a very real sense we all have our *'valley of dry bones;'* those problems that seem as though they are never going to change, maybe things we've almost given up hope on and find it really hard to see any answer to. God requires us to make a firm decision, to respond in faith affirming that our confidence is in what He is able to do. This is why Jesus said,

> *"According to your faith and trust and reliance (on the power invested in Me) be it done to you."*
>
> (Matthew 9:29b, Amp.)
>
> *"... All things are possible to him who believes."*
>
> (Mark 9:23b)

When we realise what God is able to do we are then in a position to speak with conviction and authority into dead and hopeless circumstances. Just like Ezekiel in verse 4, we can prophesy into situations that seem beyond hope and declare in faith, *"O dry bones, hear the word of the Lord!"* This man could easily have felt foolish or embarrassed speaking in such a way to a valley of dry bones, but he didn't. He simply decided to obey the prompting of God and speak out the creative, anointed Word of the Lord.

Thirdly, Respond In Faith As An Act Of Our Will

Faith is nothing whatsoever to do with feelings. If only this simple fact could be grasped, then believers would be saved from so much frustration and disappointment and the enemy would be prevented from robbing them of God's many blessings. For some Christians when they feel good they consider that they have faith and when they don't feel so bright they think they have lost their faith. In truth, faith is a choice, an act of the will to believe God independently of how we may feel and regardless of whatever circumstances we might be facing. Therefore, when God reminds us of the depth of our problems and the extent of our need, then declares what He will do, He expects us to respond and make a decision to act upon what He has said.

It would surprise many Christians today to be told that God always expects a response to His Word. He doesn't want us to debate it, nor does He expect us to discuss it. He simply requires us to choose to respond and move into what He is saying.

In looking at God's Word to the impossible and unchangeable situation of this valley full of dry bones we notice that there came a response that was **Willing - Immediate - Visible -** and **Audible.** Verse 7 says,

> *"So I prophesied as I was commanded; and as I prophesied, there was noise and behold a rattling; and the bones came together, bone to its bone."*

If there were this kind of response to God's Word whenever He spoke to us individually, or in our church meetings, we would find that revival had come. I know only too well from over twenty-five years of preaching, around this country and abroad, that sometimes I can preach my heart out at meetings and then when I give an opportunity for people to respond, those listening remain unmoved, untouched and firmly rooted to their seats!

Very often there isn't the response to God's Word that there ought to be simply because people hold back in pride and unbelief, or because of their so-called 'British Reserve.' Instead of the response we read of in verse 7, people rationalise what they hear by wondering if the promise still applies today in the same way it did when it was first spoken. For some they have no problem believing that it can happen for certain people, but unsure it could happen for them. They spend so much time wanting to examine what has been said from every angle that by the time they've made up their mind, the opportunity has passed them by! With others, they are waiting for their feelings to move them, their circumstances to be easier or until they understand things more clearly before they respond to what they have heard.

We need to hear what God is saying and decide to respond by acting upon what we know to be true. A good example of this is seen in the Bible with the blind beggar Bartimaeus. His life-changing miracle was the result of his response:

> *"And when he heard that it was Jesus of Nazareth, he began to cry out and say, "Jesus, Son of David, have mercy upon me!"* (Mark 10:47)

If he hadn't decided to do something about what he believed, then his miracle would have passed him by and he would have lost the opportunity of a finding an answer to his problem. The same was true with the woman who had a haemorrhage condition for twelve years. She was growing weaker and more tired by the day, but she believed Jesus would be the answer to her situation. She therefore decided to act upon what she believed, saying, *"... If I only touch His garment, I shall be made well."* (Matthew 9:21). The reality of her faith is seen in that she was determined to do something, and as she did, her life was changed!

Bible faith is always seen in action. This is why we read in James 2:20b, *"... Faith without works is dead."* (AV). We must choose to believe God's Word and start to respond by making some movement. This means we begin to do what we couldn't or *wouldn't* do before. We begin to think what we couldn't or *wouldn't* think before and we begin to speak what we couldn't or *wouldn't* speak before. As we start to do something in the physical realm to release our faith, something in the spirit realm is then released to us in the most wonderful way, setting in motion the miraculous power of God.

This is well illustrated in the Bible with what happened to the man who had a withered hand. He came to Jesus but the Lord didn't immediately heal him; instead he was given a word of command that required a response of obedience. Jesus said,

"Stretch out your hand." (Mark 3:5b)

It was as he began to do this he was healed! The same was true of the lame man who was brought to Jesus on a stretcher; the Lord certainly didn't instantly heal him. The command of Jesus to this man was,

"Rise, take up your pallet, and walk." (John 5:8)

When he decided to do what Jesus said he discovered he was healed. This point is probably more clearly seen with the lepers who came to Jesus. They could have felt quite offended at the Lord's words to them. They came in faith believing for healing, but it appears that Jesus dismisses them with the instructions,

"*Go and show yourselves to the priests...*" (Luke 17:14)

However, when they responded to this command the Bible tells us in the same verse, "*.... And as they went they were cleansed.*"

One other example worth considering is the fishermen who toiled all night and caught nothing. They must have felt so frustrated and discouraged by the time they came home that morning. On their return they met Jesus and instead of a word of encouragement He gave them a command that they were expected to act upon:

"*... Put out into the deep and let down your nets for a catch.*" (Luke 5:4b)

Peter's response in verse 5 was,
"*Master, we toiled all night and took nothing! But at your word I will let down the nets.*"

As these fishermen responded in faith by deciding to act upon the Word of Christ, they had the biggest catch ever in their lives! By immediately responding to God's instructions and doing something in the physical realm, their faith released the supernatural power of God. This resulted in bringing a miracle into their lives that turned their hopeless situation completely around!

In considering this principle of doing something to release faith which activates the power of God's blessing into our lives, let us look again at Ezekiel 37:7, "*... the bones came together, bone to its bone.*" We find here that each bone found a specific and a particular function in the body; they discovered where they were destined to be. There is no such thing in the body of Christ as an appendix. There are no 'spare parts' in Christ's body. The teaching Paul gives in 1 Corinthians 12 uses the analogy of a physical body to represent Christ's body the Church, and clearly shows us that each member has a part to play. Everyone has an important function and purpose and when each member is in the right place functioning, it makes bodily growth possible for the whole.

The Church will never rise to its full stature and have the impact in the community it should until this takes place. Often the problem is that the Church is full of people who do feel like 'spare parts.' They don't know their gift and ministry; that God-given role which they are to function in within the Church. For most churches today the reality is, too few are doing too much. Every member must play his or her part. We all have something to contribute to the whole. That gift might be administration, encouragement, hospitality, intercession, practical help or financially giving into the Kingdom. It could be one of the spiritual gifts mentioned in 1 Corinthians 14, or perhaps music, children's work, youth work etc. Nobody should ever feel they haven't a gift or ministry of any significance.

Therefore we need to be asking the Lord to show us what our role is in the church, and the part we ought to be playing. Then as He reveals that to us we must respond in faith as an act of our will, and begin to function out of the motive of wanting to build up and benefit the whole of the body. It is as we respond to the *'Word of the Lord'* that His enabling will be given to equip us to do what perhaps we previously considered impossible.

Fourthly, Receive The Transforming Power Of God

No matter how many times we sing the hymn *'Onward Christian Soldiers Marching As To War,'* or how enthusiastically we express the verse, *'Like A Mighty Army Moves The Church Of God!'* nothing will ever happen until we are filled with the breath of Almighty God. We need to decide that no longer are we going to struggle on in our own ability to make things work; we are finished with trying to produce what God requires in our own strength; those days are over! This is why verse 10 of Ezekiel chapter 37 is so important. Here it speaks of the breath of God coming into a prepared body:

> "... and breath entered them; they came to life and stood up on their feet – a vast army." (NIV)

Someone once said, "The Kingdom of God is not going to advance by our churches becoming filled with men, but by men, in our churches, becoming filled with God." To experience this we must come to an end of placing any confidence in our own plans, ideas and cleverly thought out strategies and become wholly reliant on His strength and power. If we are to be prepared for the day when God, once more, will pour out His Holy Spirit, our expectation must be in the Lord. This is expressed in that great hymn, written in 1878 by Edwin Hatch. The consciousness he had of his own need is voiced in this simple but sincere prayer:

> "Breathe on me, Breath of God,
> fill me with life anew.
> That I may love what thou dost love,
> and do what thou would'st do."

That's revival! When we love the things that God loves, and are doing the things that He is doing, that's revival! Without the fullness and anointing of the Holy Spirit our Christian lives will be robbed of tremendous power and ability. We remain but *'dry bones'* if the breath of God is not filling our lives! Jesus Himself required this for service. He was conceived of the Holy Spirit and walked full of the Holy Spirit, but to be fruitful and effective in His work He needed to receive power and anointing from God. This is why we read in Acts 10:38,

> "God anointed Jesus of Nazareth with the Holy Ghost and with power: who went about doing good, and healing all that were oppressed of the devil; for God was with Him." (AV)

If it was necessary for Jesus to have that special help, how much more do you and I require the same? He made clear to His disciples that they were not to attempt to serve Him in their own ability. Before they could expect to stand against the devil, make any meaningful impact upon the evil around them, and effectively proclaim the gospel, they first had to receive a unique anointing. The command of Jesus to them was,

> "Behold, I send the promise of my Father upon you; but stay in the city, until you are clothed with power from on high." (Luke 24:49)

They obeyed these instructions and on the day of Pentecost something quite extraordinary happened to them. The descriptive words that express what took place on that occasion are very significant. The Bible says,

> "And suddenly a sound came from heaven like the rush of a mighty wind, and it filled all the house where they were sitting." (Acts 2: 2)

That was the 'Breath of God,' which, in verse 4, filled everyone who was present. This wasn't isolated to just that one day though. It happened again, to the same gathering of Jewish people, in Acts 4:31, and to the Gentiles in Acts 10:44-46. These believers continued to live in the power of God's ability. It was their choice to do this that enabled those first Christians to, *'stand on their feet as an exceeding great army.'*

The apostle Paul probably saw greater miracles and experienced God's power on a daily basis more than most people ever will. Even so, his all-consuming desire and passionate prayer is seen in the overriding priority he expresses in Philippians 3:10: *"… that I may know Him, and the power of His resurrection…."* Paul walked in the supernatural power of God and encouraged others to do the same. One of the many remarkable statements he made was to the Christians at Rome. To them he said,

> *"If the Spirit of Him who raised up Jesus from the dead dwells in you, He that raised up Christ from the dead shall also quicken your mortal bodies by His Spirit that dwelleth in you."* (Romans 8:11)

That same resurrection power is available today and it will always bring a *"quickening"* to our mortal bodies, not merely when we die, but now in life! There was unmistakable evidence of this for all to see in Paul's life. He expected that same evidence to be just as clear in the lives of others who were walking in the power of the resurrection. When someone is filled with the power and breath of God you won't be left puzzling as to whether or not they are; you'll know it! This was the confidence Paul had when he spoke to the Christians at Corinth:

> *"… my speech and my message were not in plausible words of wisdom, but in demonstration of the Spirit and of power."* (1Corinthians 2:4)

There is, at times, much talk among Pentecostals as to what is the initial evidence of being filled with the Holy Spirit. Some would argue that speaking with *'other tongues'* is that evidence, but such a position is ridiculous because even false cults and sects today do this. We need to get back to our bibles and rather than drawing conclusions from conjecture on this matter, we must see the black and white statement of Acts 1:8. This says, *"But <u>you shall receive power</u> when the Holy Spirit has come upon you; and <u>you shall</u> <u>be my witnesses</u>...."* Supernatural boldness to share the gospel and be a witness is that initial evidence! Some Christians today may speak with *"other tongues"* and yet never talk of Jesus to those that need to be saved. How we need courage today to stand and speak out for Christ. C.T. Studd in his book 'Chocolate Soldiers' wrote these challenging words:

> "Heroism is the lost chord; the missing note of present day Christianity! Every true soldier is a hero! **A Soldier Without Heroism Is A Chocolate Soldier!** Who has not been stirred to scorn and mirth at the very thought of a Chocolate Soldier? In peace time true soldiers are like captive lions, fretting in their cages. War gives them their liberty and sends them, like boys bounding out of school, to obtain their heart's desire or perish in the attempt. Battle is the soldier's vital breath! Peace turns him into a stooping asthmatic. War makes him a whole man again, and gives him the heart, strength, and vigour of a hero."

In addition to this unmistakable evidence of boldness, other clear signs will be seen in those filled with the breath of God. For example: (a) Greater joy and liberty in praise and worship. (b) Release into the dimension of supernatural gifts of the Spirit. (c) Deeper commitment to the Lord and motivation towards service within the Church. (d) Greater passion for prayer, the Bible and Jesus Himself, and (e) an acceleration of Spiritual growth and maturity.

One of the reasons why these clear signs are not often seen in the lives of believers is because they settle down in an experience that was in the past and have no present day reality of what once was so meaningful. That experience of God's blessing might have been wonderful at the time, but if we try to live off yesterday's provision we soon become very dry. The attitude of every believer needs to be the same as that of Paul who said:

> *"Not that I have already obtained this or am already perfect, but I press on to make it my own...."*
>
> (Philippians 3:12)

We must be always pressing on and pressing in to the fullness of everything that God has to give us.

The only way, therefore, to prepare for 'the day of God's power', is by choosing to humble ourselves and make a decision to seriously do whatever it takes to be ready for Him to use us. The key is found in Psalm 110:3a where it says,

"Your people will offer themselves <u>willingly</u> in the day of your power…" (Amp.)

We must be willing to:

Firstly - **Recognise** our true condition before a Holy God.

Secondly - **Realise** what He is able to do, both for us, and through us, to reach others.

Thirdly - **Respond** to His Word in faith as a decisive act of our will.

Fourthly - **Receive** the supernatural, transforming power of God's Spirit.

The matter of being willing to make right decisions, pleasing to God, is ours alone. It is one that nobody else can make for us. This is true, not only regarding the specific area of preparing for revival; it is also the case with every topic raised throughout this book. The emphasis in relation to each of the chapters we've considered has been the fundamental fact that, **Decisions Determine Your Destiny!** May God help each one of us in our daily choices, as we live our lives for His glory, and the benefit of others.

Other Publications By Yan Hadley

Available From
New Life Publications
45 Heatherbrook Road
Anstey Heights
Leicester LE4 1AL

Telephone: 0116 235 6992
E-mail: newlife.hadley@ntlworld.com

REAPING GOD'S HARVEST @ £3.99 + p&p
(Equipping the Church for Evangelism)

Yan's aim in this book is to stimulate faith in the lives of every believer to discover the ability of sharing Christ with others. Through practical teaching and personal illustrations evangelism is seen to be, not only a responsibility, but also a privilege and joy.

ANSWERING TODAY'S PROBLEMS @ £4.99 + p&p
(Helping Ourselves to Help Others)

This book shows clearly God's answer to some common problems in life today. People will find help not only for themselves, but also insight into being able to help others.

CONSISTENT CHRISTIAN LIVING @ £3.50 + p&p
(Four Keys to Remaining in Victory)

Many Christians find it difficult to accept that they can live consistently with joy, fulfilment and victory. In this book Yan writes to lift the expectancy of every believer to think differently. A life of consistency is seen to be normal and not merely for a select few.

REALISING YOUR FULL POTENTIAL @ £6.99 + p&p
This publication has the purpose of encouraging people to discover the greatness of God in their lives. It makes clear that every believer, even the most unlikely, is able to be used by God in a very significant way.

Why not visit our website: www.newlifeministrytrust.com